# Crappie Fly-Fishing

## A Seasonal Approach

**Terry & Roxanne Wilson**

Illustrated by John "Lefty" Wilson

**Frank Amato Publications**

Portland, Oregon
www.AmatoBooks.com

All inquiries should be addressed to:
Frank Amato Publications, Inc.
P.O. Box 82112
Portland, Oregon 97282
(503) 653-8108 • www.AmatoBooks.com

Illustrations by John "Lefty" Wilson
ISBN-13: 978-1-57188-500-5
UPC: 0-81127-00346-4
Printed in China

10 9 8 7 6 5 4 3 2 1

# Table Of Contents

# Acknowledgements

Decades of pursuing crappies with fly rods have enabled them to teach us about their needs, preferences, habits, and lifestyles; but much of our knowledge has also come from professional guides and the many crappie enthusiasts with whom we've shared the sport from all corners of the crappies' range. Fly shop owners, fly tiers, rod builders, conservation officers, and fisheries biologists have all contributed to these pages. We are indebted to each, even those whose names have been forgotten long before this project was considered.

Writing this book has been a labor of love and we have these generous folks to thank for enhancing our efforts. Their help, advice, and encouragement has facilitated its completion and enhanced our enjoyment of this project:

John "Lefty" Wilson, who sees the crappie's world uniquely through the eyes of an accomplished artist and an adept fly-fisher. His illustrations have always beautifully supplemented our words. It was he who first encouraged us to write nearly thirty years ago.

Larry Offner, owner of The Green Trout Fly Shop in Baton Rouge, Louisiana, for encouraging, insisting actually, that we write this book.

Dail Graham, owner of The Eagle's Nest Resort on Missouri's Lake Pomme de Terre, for sharing his knowledge of crappie locations, his flies, and methods.

Rex and Diane Warren for sharing their pond where catching giant crappies is always possible.

Rob Woodruff, guide, entomologist, and writer, whose knowledge and guiding skills are always so agreeably given on the waters of east Texas.

The late Delmas Norcross, whose invitation to share a private lake so many years ago triggered our interest in crappies.

Ron Kruger for sharing his knowledge of crappies and guiding us on the waters of Kentucky Lake.

Charlie Reading, owner of Reading's Fly Shop near Missouri's Bennett Spring State Park, for sharing his knowledge of fly-fishing and the products that enhance our sport.

Marc Pinsel for sharing time on the water hunting crappies and for his elegant streamers.

Kyle Moppert for sharing his fly patterns and his thoughts and love of warmwater species, especially Chinquapin.

Tom Conry for advice on professional graphics.

Special thanks to the Federation of Fly-fishers for providing the forum for discussion of warmwater issues and conservation, and for assisting in the education of warmwater fly-fishers and fly tiers.

# Crappie Hunters

For over a quarter century Terry and Roxanne Wilson have presented practical, innovative fly-fishing methods for bluegill, largemouth and smallmouth bass, crappie, shortnose gar, and channel catfish in over 200 magazine articles published in *Flyfishing and Tying Journal, The Flyfisher, Midwest Fly Fishing, Warmwater Flyfishing, Fly Fishing Quarterly, Bassmaster, Ontario Out-of-Doors, A Tight Loop*, and many others. They are staff writers for St. Louis-based *Outdoor Guide Magazine* and write the Fly-fishing column for *Driftwood Outdoors*. The Wilsons have travelled widely to share their enthusiasm and methods through seminars, demonstrations and presentations at club meetings; outdoor shows; state, regional, and international fly-fishing shows.

Terry's original flies for bluegill, largemouth bass, smallmouth bass, and crappies have been featured in *Fly Fish America, Flyfishing and Tying Journal, Popular Flyfishing, The Flyfisher*, and *Eastern Fly Fishing* and have been included in the books, *Innovative Flies and Techniques* (c2005), and The Federation of Flyfishers' *Fly Pattern Encyclopedia* (c2000). His flies are available through Orvis, Pacific Fly Group, and their website www.thebluegillpond.com, as well as selected fly shops. Roxanne's photography accompanies their magazine articles, books, website, and presentations.

The Wilsons' first book, **Bluegill Fly-Fishing & Flies**, was published in 1999 by Frank Amato Publications, Inc. Their second book, **Largemouth Bass Fly-Fishing: Beyond the Basics**, also published by Frank Amato Publications, Inc., was released in 2001. **Smallmouth Bass Fly-Fishing: A Practical Guide** was published in 2007. **Crappie Fly-Fishing: A Seasonal Approach** is their fourth book. (see page 112)

Terry and Roxanne are active life members of the Federation of Fly Fishers. They were presented with the Don Harger Memorial Award in 1996 for their contributions to the sport of fly-fishing. They are also members of the Missouri Smallmouth Alliance and serve on the Board of Directors for the Missouri Outdoor Writers Association.

The Wilsons live in southwest Missouri where they enjoy fishing the streams, lakes, and ponds of the Ozark Mountains.

# Introduction

Once upon a time crappies were accidental hookups as we cast for bluegills or largemouth bass. But that changed one April evening when, at a friend's invitation, we fished a private pond loaded with what he called "Strawberry Bass." We were surprised to discover they were crappies but there was no time for reflection as nearly every cast produced a lusty hit. Often when we missed the strike another fish would immediately grab the fly. The fun continued until dark when we cased our rods and retreated to a nearby café. There it was explained that the fabulous fishing was only a spring phenomenon. After the spawn the crappies retreated to deep water and were nearly impossible to catch because they became semi-dormant.

Unfortunately for many that notion persists and in the process some of the year's finest fishing is forsaken. This is particularly true of fly-fishers that regard their presentations as suitable only for the shallows. Catching crappies shouldn't end when the spawn is finished. In the decades since that remarkable trip we've fished year round for crappies. We've picked the brains of many of the country's best crappie guides, compiled their information and advice, then translated the information gleaned from spin-casters to the use of fly-fishers.

After the publication of our first book, *Bluegill Fly-fishing and Flies* Frank Amato Publications, 1999, we were asked when we would write a book about crappies. After years of experimentation, interviews, research, and the encouragement of many fly-fishers we have completed the project. In these pages we've sought to tell you where to locate crappies in all seasons in consideration of weather in natural lakes, sprawling impoundments, ponds, strip-mine pits, rivers, creeks, bayous, and oxbows. In addition we've discussed selecting flies for each of the specific presentations we've recommended. We want to pass along all that we have learned from our discussions with guides, our own trial and error, successes and frustrations, good luck and perseverance. In the process it's our hope that you will catch a lot more crappies and enjoy it as much as we do.

## Chapter 1

# Understanding Crappies: America's Favorite Gamefish?

An excellent case can be made that crappies are America's most popular gamefish. After all, they are pursued by nearly all anglers of all ages using every manner of fish-catching method from cane poles and bobbers to the most sophisticated electronically equipped bass boat that costs tens of thousands. Surely there must be a reason for their remarkable popularity. Actually, there are many. First is the crappie's adaptability, as they take up residence in huge reservoirs, natural lakes, community lakes, ponds, abandoned strip-mine pits, drainage ditches, canals, sloughs, rivers, creeks, bayous, and even brackish tidal waters. Their original range stretched from southern Canada and the Great Lakes to Florida and from Nebraska to the Gulf of Mexico. Now, through stocking, crappies are at home in all of the contiguous 48 states and Hawaii, plus southern Canada and Mexico. They form a catchable population that thrives in deep, clear water as well as weed-choked bays and chocolate-colored mud holes.

Of equal importance, crappies are prolific spawners and are therefore abundant, sometimes to their own detriment. They are capable of reproducing at such a rapid rate that without adequate predation in smaller waters they quickly overpopulate, thus stunting frequently results. One study indicates that some female crappies deposit only 20 to 30 percent of their eggs, but this may relate to population dynamics or disruptions to the spawn due to weather changes. Cold fronts can affect water temperatures at a time when two or three degrees determine whether the fish remain on relatively shallow spawning nests or retreat to staging areas in deeper water. Most crappies are sexually mature at two years, and most first-time spawning females produce 20,000 to 30,000 eggs while older, larger specimens are capable of depositing 150,000 eggs. Even when considering the devastation of fluctuating water levels, as can occur in big reservoirs and radical water temperature changes due to cold fronts or heavy predation, the odds of a sizeable hatch are excellent.

A third reason for the crappie's popularity is that they are voracious, competitive feeders. Once located they are easily enticed to bite and often

*The crappie's soft mouth is easily torn by hard hook-sets.*

aren't particularly choosy about the menu. They are a schooling fish, and consequently must compete with each other in order to satisfy their appetites. It's very much like growing up in a large family. At the dinner table the most aggressive siblings leave with their hunger satisfied while more reticent members of the clan are left wanting more. This competitive mentality is very much to the advantage of anglers because the opportunity to catch many fish is a strong inducement that attracts lots of fans.

Another consideration is that crappies put up a strong fight that's quite sporting on appropriate tackle. Their soft mouths make horsing them impossible while they pull vigorously. It's a delicate operation to land crappies of size and a soft rod is helpful to enhance the fight. Some anglers may downplay the fight of any fish weighing only a half pound, but the truth of the matter is that the fight of a 10-pound bass wouldn't be anything special if it was landed on a rod meant to subdue giant tuna or marlin. It's the use of sporting equipment that makes a good fight. Put a 10- or 11-inch crappie on a medium action 3- or 4-weight fly rod and even the most jaded angler must admit to having his hands full.

The speckled black and silver-white body of the crappie, with its oversized dorsal and anal fins, makes the species a natural beauty. In the water the colorful fins and tail undulate gently like a flag waving in a gentle breeze. If beauty is the standard by which gamefish are judged then the crappie ranks near the top of any list.

Yet another reason for the crappie's immense popularity is that it is regarded by many as freshwater's most palatable fish. Although bones can be problematic on smaller species, larger fish can be filleted to eliminate most of the problem. Most of the fine bones soften or dissolve altogether when cooked. The white flesh can be prepared according to a variety of recipes, from barbequed to fried in beer batter. Crappies have probably provisioned more shore lunches than any other freshwater gamefish.

Clearly there are many compelling reasons to pursue this great gamefish, but why, with so many choices of methods available to the angler, would the instrument of choice be a fly rod? Just as there are a number of reasons for crappie popularity, choice of the fly rod is based on several points of sound reasoning.

## Why Use A Fly Rod?

The best reason for using a fly rod in the pursuit of crappies is that it's more fun. That long, limber wand bounces with each tug of the fish's efforts to avoid capture. Why not employ the most enjoyable means of catching the fish? The fly rod encourages active participation because anglers are actively pursuing the bite rather than waiting for it to occur. For this reason alone the choice of using a fly rod for crappies is a no-brainer. The joy of the cast, with its rhythmic flowing of line, forces the caster to slow down and relax. If the cast is hurried, line cascades in inglorious loops and coils. The act of fly-casting, unlike any other form of angling, injects added enjoyment into the pursuit of fish. Having employed nearly every manner of fish-capturing, it is our conclusion that the enjoyment of all other methods is dependent upon the actual catching of fish. Among the benefits of fly-casting is that at least part of the fun comes from the act of delivering the fly. Another reason to use the long rod is that on an appropriately sized outfit the thrashing fight and mad dashes of each crappie are accentuated. Not only does this relate to the fun of each fish encounter, but in a more pragmatic sense it enables the fly-fisher to understand where the crappie is trying to go in his efforts to escape so he can reach a brush pile or weedbed. Clearly the long, limber fly rod accentuates the fight and requires more from the angler than brute strength to subdue the fish.

In fighting crappies, the tissue-thin tissue of their mouths must constantly be taken into consideration. A stout hook-set often tears the soft parts of the fish's mouth, which allows the hook to pull free. The fly rod, with its soft, springy action, provides a gentler hook-set that results in fewer lost fish. Another argument favoring the use of the fly rod is that it is capable of delivering the fly to the water with the delicacy of a whisper. With virtually any other presentation method there is a considerable splash-down that can easily scare shallow fish that are making their initial foray into the spawning grounds after spending a long winter in the protection of deeper water.

The fly rod was originally conceived as a tool for delivering insect imitations. Insects, both as emergent adults perched on the water's surface and in their subaquatic nymph stage, comprise a major part of the crappie's diet. Other presentations ignore insect replication entirely, yet the fly rod lacks nothing in the presentation of minnow or crustacean imitations. In fact, by utilizing streamers, fly rod jigs or many other fly possibilities the complete selection of dietary interests of the crappie can be presented in a manner superior to any other method.

### The Hook-Set

The flexible fly rod offers an advantage in hook-setting as well. The thin flesh of the crappie's mouth is easily torn, thus a hard hook-set is enough to lose the catch, yet if the hook-set doesn't come quickly enough the fly will be rejected. In general a quick lifting of the rod tip will do the trick, but fishing at increased depths can change that. While the quick lift will get the job done in shallow water to a depth of perhaps five feet, a firmer lift is required at 10 feet, and a lift that's firmer still is required at 15 to 20 feet. Another escape possibility for the hooked crappie is that the hole created by hook penetration is easily enlarged during the tug-of-war fight. The longer the crappie is played the more likely the fish will be able to gain freedom. Lost fish also occur when anglers lift their newly-caught crappies to hand, straining leaders and tippets, or when they lift and swing the fish to them. The landing method works—part of the time. A far better plan is using a landing net regardless of whether you're fishing from shore, wading, float tubing or in a boat.

In consideration of all the advantages of using a fly rod in the pursuit of crappies the real question is not, "Why use the long rod?" but more appropriately, "Why not?" There is no conventional-tackle presentation that cannot be replicated with the fly rod, most often in a superior manner with more productive results.

## Bill's "Giant" Crappie

Fly-fishing seems to create a more conservation-friendly group of sportsmen. With that concept in mind we were introduced to Bill, a community newcomer anxious to win over a base of support for his new position as local school superintendent and, as it turns out, to enhance his fishing opportunities.

"How's the fishing in this area?" Bill asked.

"Very good," we answered nearly in unison. "We fly-fish local ponds and lakes for bluegill, crappie, and bass."

Bill beamed broadly, "Oh, wonderful! So do I."

The furniture had barely been unloaded from Bill's moving van when we pulled into his driveway to guide him to a large watershed pond in the hills near town. Bill emerged from the garage carrying an ancient bamboo fly rod that easily qualified as the most abused fishing utensil we'd ever seen. Chunks of the cork handle were missing and taped together. An equally decrepit spinning reel was attached to the reel seat with black electrical tape and misaligned guides were crudely retied with coarse thread covered in sloppily applied epoxy. The tip of the rod was broken off, leaving three inches of exposed cane and the next guide to serve as the monofilament line's last contact with the rod. A big red and white bobber wobbled at mid-rod as Bill approached our jeep and boat trailer.

"Boy, if this rod could talk," Bill enthused as he climbed aboard.

One of us recalls thinking that it would probably be screaming about the horrors it had endured.

With the spawn long past we had been catching some of the 25-acre pond's big crappie near submerged cedar trees in eight to 10 feet of water. Using the trolling motor we maneuvered into position and invited our guest to drop his minnow-tipped jig into the water. Action came immediately. A 10-inch bass and two small crappies were lifted into the boat and released before Bill's bobber completely disappeared into the depths. The much-damaged rod bent dramatically while creaking audibly with its top few inches piercing the water's surface. Eventually, to Bill's great delight we netted an enormous crappie. That's when things began to deteriorate. Holding his venerated rod in one hand he affixed his prize to a heavy metal stringer and leaned over the

gunnel to clip it to an oar lock. Bill leaned a bit too far over the gunnel. To our astonishment he somersaulted over the side, grasping the ancient rod in one hand and the stringer in the other. Sputtering for breath, he emerged at the boat's side with coontail and duck weed draped across his head and shoulders and held onto the gunnel while we paddled and poled him into the nearest shallow shoreline. The rod with all the stories to tell was firmly in Bill's grasp with yet another survival tale and doubtless several more scars along its length, but the stringer and giant crappie were not. While still clinging to the side of the boat and even before emerging from the water, Bill bemoaned the loss of the giant crappie.

"I wanted to have it mounted," he whined, "That was my biggest fish ever."

Regrets continued as he stumbled ashore and sprawled onto the bank to recover from his ordeal. He was far more upset about losing the fish than about any injury he might have incurred. Against our better judgment, the one of us with a surplus of testosterone stripped naked and dog paddled to the scene of the crime. On the third dive the metal stringer was hoisted overhead and dragged ashore.

"I think I'll retire my old rod and hang it above my 'Moby Dick'," Bill gushed.

That should have been the end of the story, but it wasn't.

At an academic awards banquet a few months later, Bill's wife thanked us for recovering Bill's fish, adding, "It was delicious."

The desire to inflict bodily harm has never been greater.

### A Little Taxonomy And A Lot Of Aliases

The name "crappie" (pronounced CROP-ee) is derived from the French word "crapet-soleil," which means "sunfish." They are members of the sunfish family *Centrarchidae* which also includes largemouth and smallmouth bass, rock bass, bluegills, redears, green sunfish, and numerous other species. This family shares several important characteristics that include a generally flattened body, large eyes, and spines in their dorsal and anal fins. Crappies are also the only members of the genus *Pomoxis*, and there is not one crappie but two: white crappie (*Pomoxis annularis)* and black crappie (*Pomoxis nigromaculatus)*. While they share many physical characteristics there are also some readily recognizable differences. The white crappie's body displays vertical bars along its side while the black crappie's sides feature a dense, irregularly speckled appearance. The white crappie has five or six dorsal spines while the black crappie has seven or eight. Crappies that are taken from clear water tend to be more easily identified because their markings are more pronounced, but those from dark water are less distinct. To further complicate the identification process their ranges often overlap and hybridization often occurs. Offspring display characteristics of both parents.

In general black crappies tend to inhabit cool, clear water mostly located in the northern portion of its range while white crappies are more at home in warmer, more turbid southern waters. Yet black crappies dominate in Florida's lakes and streams and they are more common in the brackish tidal river mouths of the southeastern coast.

Whichever of the crappie species is dominant in your waters you can bet that they have more aliases than a cell block full of con artists. Some of these nicknames are descriptive of one or the other of the species. White crappies, for example, are referred to as "silver crappie," "white perch," and "pale crappie" to name a few, while their black cousins are called "calico," "strawberry bass," or "speckled perch." Some of their unusual monikers are specific to various areas of the country. In New England, for example, crappie may be known as "millpond bass" while crappie enthusiasts in Louisiana might refer to them as "sac-a-lait" (pronounced sack-a-lay), which is Cajun French and roughly translates as "sack of milk," referring to the crappie's delicate white flesh or as "Chinquapin" (pronounced chink-a-pin), which is an Algonquian native

American word. It refers to a type of chestnut tree, but in Louisiana any generally round or saucer-shaped sunfish is branded with the nickname.

In the early 1970's Don Gapen wrote that the U.S. Department of Interior published a book titled *Sportfishing U.S.A.* in which they identified 55 names used by anglers to refer to crappies. In addition to those listed by the Interior Department there are many more nicknames. This list, nevertheless, is interesting even if incomplete.

| | | | |
|---|---|---|---|
| Bachelor | Calico Bass | Newlight | Spotted Perch |
| Crapet | Calico Bream | Papermouth | Spotted Trout |
| Pale Crappie | Campbellite | Perch | Straw Bass |
| Ringed Crappie | Chinquapin | Razorback | Strawberry Bass |
| Timber Crappie | Chinquapin Perch | Roach | Strawberry Perch |
| Bachelor Perch | Dolly Varden | Sac-a-lait | Suckley Perch |
| Bachelor Shad | Goggle-Eye | Rockfish | Sun Perch |
| Banklick | Goggle-Eye Perch | Sago | Tin Mouth |
| Banklick Bass | Goldring | Silver Bass | Tin Perch |
| Barfish | Grass Bass | Silver Perch | White Perch |
| Bigfin Bass | John Demon | Shad | |
| Butterhead | Lake Bass | Sand Perch | |
| Bridge Perch | Lake Erie Bass | Speckled Bass | |
| Bride Perch | Lamplighter | Speckled Perch | |
| Calico | Millpond Bass | Speck | |

Add to this impressive list further nicknames such as "slabs," "slabbies," "old silver sides," and "silvers," and we begin to understand the unique affection these terms of endearment are meant to convey. But irrespective of the name we apply to them we must come to understand their dietary needs and be able to apply that knowledge to the waters we fish in order to be consistently successful in their capture.

## The Crappie's Menu

As a highly adaptable species crappie depend upon what is available to them. As a result it is difficult to classify them as either very selective or non-discriminatory feeders. It depends entirely on their environment. What is consumed also depends on the crappie's size, the most available prey, and the time of year. Most young-of-the-year crappies feed on zooplankton.

As crappies grow, small insect larvae and emergent insects become important. Eventually small fish become an important part of the crappie's diet.

In spring when small fish are less available adult crappies focus their attention on plankton and aquatic insects, but as the season evolves into summer the young-of-the-year hatchlings from a variety of species, including the crappies' offspring, become the primary food source in most waters. The abundance of summer continues into autumn as small fish continue to dominate the crappies' attention. The cold-water temperatures of winter reduce their metabolism and their need to feed, but they continue to take small fish when they can and return to subaquatic insects and plankton when necessary.

In large reservoirs of the mid-South and South the forage base is primarily gizzard or threadfin shad. This reliable, abundant food source enables crappies to feed heavily on them and the resulting growth rates can be remarkable. Eventually young shad outgrow their usefulness as a primary food source so crappies must then return to insects, minnows, and small crustaceans to fill the void. Despite their predilection for smaller food forms, a local crappie guide reports dressing several crappies each season that have ingested shad that are half their length. Ten-inch crappies, for example, had five-inch shad folded into their stomachs. This guide, a southeastern Louisiana native Cajun, has some sage advice for those wishing to target monster crappies. He advises the use of "baits" up to five inches long and a 3/0 or 4/0 hook. He further warns that you are not likely to catch a limit of 14- to 17-inchers but you may well catch the biggest crappie of your life.

On the natural lakes of the northern portion of its range, shad are less likely to be available. In this case the focus of the adult crappie diet is young-of-the-year bass, perch, bluegill, minnows, and their own fry. These species, too, will outgrow their role as prey which forces crappies to return to aquatic insects, minnows, and crustaceans.

## The Dominant Year Class

Anglers are often confused by dramatic fluctuations in the crappie population from year to year. They blame overfishing, too many predator fish, pollution or even a fish kill. Often these fish population changes are actually caused by the crappies themselves. When spawning conditions are not adversely affected by weather or drastic water level changes and food is plentiful, the crappie spawn is exceptionally successful, which produces an extremely large hatch of young fish known as the dominant year class. In succeeding years, this dominant class devours its own young to the point that there are many fewer fish in those year classes. Eventually the dominant class begins to lose numbers due to natural causes, as well as fishing pressure. In time the original dominant year class is no longer capable of removing most of the yearly hatch. When that occurs and conditions are again conducive to a good hatch another dominant year class is produced and the cycle continues. When the population of the dominant class is at its peak anglers can catch limits of mid-sized fish rather easily, but very few specimens will achieve bragging status. A couple of seasons later limits may be hard to fill, but many of those that are caught will be very large fish. The following season may produce large numbers of undersized fish.

The cyclical nature of the dominant year class is not the reason for stunted crappies. That is attributable to environmental factors including geographic location, water temperature, available food, competition for food, and available habitat. This range of reasons can cause a wide variance in growth rates from year to year even in the same water. In the simplest terms stunting is most often the product of too many fish and too little food.

## Crappie Behavior

The crappie's flat body enables quick, tight turns, which is particularly advantageous in brush and weeds. Like most predators its eyes are set high on its narrow head which foretells of its decided preference for feeding on prey that are located above its position. Its large eyes are also light-sensitive, which is an indication to anglers that, especially in clear water, crappies feed most actively in low-light conditions. It also forces them deeper in the water column during sun lit periods of the day.

In expansive reservoirs and natural lakes crappies move about, sometimes for considerable distances, to locate suitable food sources as well as to find comfortable temperatures. This nomadic tendency is also part of their lifestyle in rivers. Once a suitable area has been located they may remain in that general area until either the food source moves or is substantially diminished. A change in the water temperature is a strong signal to both the prey species and the crappies that a major relocation is necessary.

Both species of crappie are "schooling" fish which means that their tendency is to spend time grouped together, usually within their own year class. Often some of these schools or pods of fish are tightly confined within large brush piles but they may also form more loosely organized schools

*Black crappie prefer vegetation and less turbidity than white crappie, but the two species often interbreed.*

while suspended over deep water. The schooling tendency creates a need for them to feed competitively, which is responsible for their reputation as aggressive biters. Schooling is also a great advantage for anglers because, once located, it is possible to catch many in the same area. At times this is unfortunate because heavy fishing pressure can be responsible for removing so many fish that on some bodies of water the population balance between predator and prey is adversely affected and fishing success is diminished for years to come.

In addition to being a school fish crappie in many waters spend considerable amounts of time suspended. That is to say that they may be located at 12 feet beneath the surface, for example, over a 30-foot bottom. In this condition crappies tend to school horizontally so that most are located at the same depth. A large school can be spread over a considerable area. Many times this phenomenon is because the water temperature is more comfortable than at other depths, but it may also relate to their forage base. It may, for example, be the depth of the shad population or a particular minnow species. It may also be the depth at which zooplankton is located, which is largely a product of light intensity. Some of these plankton species rise when light is low and go deeper when light penetration is extensive. This at least gives the angler one piece to the puzzle of helping to locate suspended crappies, but looking out at the extensive open water of any large lake or river can be intimidating. Are there other clues that can help anglers locate suspended fish? Fortunately, the answer is yes.

## Understanding Open Water

Not all open water is created equal. True open water is that great expanse of water that is unrelated to any shoreline or even mid-lake structure such as humps or islands. It takes a powerful, specialized body for a fish species to survive here. Chinook and coho salmon are examples of species that have the bodies to prosper in true open water, as do striped bass and lake trout.

The crappie does not. Their body shape is adapted for maneuvering in tight quarters, yet they spend considerable amounts of time suspended over deep water. The areas in which crappies choose to suspend are not in these true open-water areas, but instead in areas with boundaries. These contained areas are found at the mouths of coves or between islands and shores. On large waters the area may be several hundred yards wide, yet this confined open water gives crappies a comfortable boundary with which to relate. This helps narrow the search for suspended crappies considerably and provides the angler

*After the spawn look for suspended crappies in confined open water.*

with a major piece of the crappie location puzzle. Simply by recognizing the time of day and angle of sunlight penetration or lack thereof, anglers can fish either relatively shallow or deep, depending upon light penetration on the narrowing at the mouths of coves with the reasonable expectation of encountering crappies. Often crappies suspended in confined open water appear to be resting. They may be feeding on plankton that is brought to their positions by wind currents. It's rare when they chase a meal from this position but jig flies and nymphs suspended directly overhead can entice them to hit. The deeper their suspended position the more reluctant they are to strike. The choice of utilizing these areas of confined open water is applicable to relatively small bodies of water as well as gigantic reservoirs. When crappies are suspended, look for them in confined open water.

America's favorite freshwater gamefish is most efficiently pursued with a fly rod. The fish that is known by many nicknames is at home in the brush but spends considerable time suspended over relatively deep water while feeding on insect life and small fish. Its growth is relatively fast and it can reach a pretty respectable size (several state records exceed 5 pounds). (See Table 1-A). It is an aggressive, competitive feeder that lives in schools, so that once located by anglers crappies can be caught in good numbers. The angler must take on the role of a hunter and learn the nuances of crappie behavior season by season for consistent success.

# State Record Crappies (Table 1A)

Many states do not differentiate between White Crappies and Black Crappies in keeping data for their state-record catches. State records listed here that were simply labeled "Crappie" are marked with an asterisk (*).

## White Crappie

| State | Weight | Place | Date |
|---|---|---|---|
| Alabama | 4 lbs. 9 oz. | Martin Lake | 5/8/2000 |
| Arizona | 3 lbs. 5.28 oz. | Lake Pleasant | 2/22/1982 |
| Arkansas | 4 lb. 7 oz. | Big Mingo Creek | 4/12/1993 |
| California | 4 lbs. 8 oz. | Clear Lake | 4/26/1971 |
| Colorado | 4 lbs. 3.75 oz. | Northglenn Lake | 4/3/1975 |
| Connecticut | 4.0 lbs. | Pataganset Lake | 1974 |
| Delaware* | | | |
| Florida* | | | |
| Georgia | 5 lbs. 0 oz. | Private pond | 4/10/1984 |
| Idaho | 3 lbs. 8.8 oz. | Crane Creek Reservoir | 7/9/2007 |
| Illinois | 4 lbs 7 oz. | Private pond | 4/8/1973 |
| Indiana* | | | |
| Iowa* | | | |
| Kansas | 4 lbs. 0.25 oz. | Private pond Greenwood County | 3/30/1964 |
| Kentucky* | | | |
| Louisiana | 3.25 lbs. | Bar pit | 2/1999 |
| Maine | N/A | | |
| Maryland* | | | |
| Massachusetts* | | | |
| Michigan | 3.39 lbs. | Stony Creek Lake | 2000 |
| Minnesota | 3 lbs. 15 oz. | Constance Lake | 7/28/2002 |
| Mississippi | 5 lbs. 3 oz. | Enid Reservoir | 7/31/1957 |
| Missouri | 5.02 lbs. | Private pond Callaway County | 4/21/2006 |

# White Crappie

| State | Weight | Place | Date |
|---|---|---|---|
| Montana* | | | |
| Nebraska | 4 lbs. 1 oz. | Red Willow Reservoir | 5/18/1980 |
| Nevada | 2 lbs. 13 oz. | Weber Reservoir | 6/4/2000 |
| New Hampshire | N/A | | |
| New Jersey | 3 lbs. 11 oz. | Mercer Lake | 5/2/2009 |
| New Mexico | N/A | | |
| New York | 3 lbs. 13 oz. | Sleepy Hollow Lake | 6/9/2001 |
| North Carolina | 3 lbs. 12 oz. | Tar River Reservoir | 4/6/2010 |
| North Dakota* | | | |
| Ohio | 3.9 lbs. | Private pond | 4/25/1995 |
| Oklahoma | 4 lbs. 15 oz. | Private pond | 5/4/1991 |
| Oregon | 4 lbs. 12 oz. | Gerber Reservoir | 1967 |
| Pennsylvania* | | | |
| Rhode Island | N/A | | |
| South Carolina | 5 lbs. 1 oz. | Lake Murray | 1949 |
| South Dakota | 3 lbs. 9 oz. | Private pond | 4/28/1974 |
| Tennessee | 5 lbs. 1 oz. | pond Dickson County | 4/20/1968 |
| Texas | 4.56 lbs. | Navarro Mills | 2/14/1968 |
| Utah | N/A | | |
| Vermont | 3 lbs. 8.5 oz. | N/A | N/A |
| Virginia* | | | |
| Washington | 2.8 lbs. | Columbia River-Burbank Slough | 7/21/1988 |
| West Virginia* | | | |
| Wisconsin | 3 lbs. 13.1 oz. | Cranberry Marsh | 5/4/2003 |
| Wyoming | 2 lbs. 5 oz. | Glendo Reservoir | 2000 |

# Black Crappie

| State | Weight | Place | Date |
|---|---|---|---|
| Alabama | 4 lbs. 5 oz. | Fort Payne Reservoir | 3/27/2007 |
| Arizona | 4 lbs. 10 oz. | San Carlos Lake | 1959 |
| Arkansas | 4 lbs. 9 oz. | Oladale Lake | 3/29/1976 |
| California | 4 lbs. 1 oz. | New Hogan Lake | 3/29/1975 |
| Colorado | 3 lbs. 4 oz. | Private pond | 1990 |
| Connecticut | 2 lbs. 12.8 oz. | Bellamy Reservoir | 2/9/2000 |
| Delaware * | 4 lbs. 9 oz. | Noxontown Pond | 5/30/1976 |
| Florida * | 3 lbs. 13 oz. | Lake Talquin | 1/21/1992 |
| Georgia | 4 lbs. 4 oz.<br>4 lbs. 4 oz. | Acrees Lake<br>Lake Spivey | 6/1/1971<br>3/1/1975 |
| Idaho | 3 lbs. 8.96 oz. | Brownlee Reservoir | 6/8/2003 |
| Illinois | 4 lbs. 8 oz. | Rend Lake | 5/15/1976 |
| Indiana * | 4 lbs. 11 oz. | Private pond | 1994 |
| Iowa * | 4 lbs. 9 oz. | Green Castle Lake | 5/1981 |
| Kansas | 4 lbs. 10 oz. | Woodson Lake | 10/21/1957 |
| Kentucky * | 4 lbs. 14 oz. | Watershed Lake | 10/21/1957 |
| Louisiana | 3.21 lbs. | Williams Canal | 2/1996 |
| Maine | 3 lbs. 4 oz. | N/A | 12/28/1986 |
| Maryland * | 4 lbs. 7 oz. | Farm pond | 5/30/2004 |
| Massachusetts * | 4 lbs. 10 oz. | Jakes Pond | 1980 |
| Michigan | 4.12 lbs. | Lincoln Lake | 1947 |
| Minnesota | 5 lbs. 0 oz. | Vermillion River | 1940 |
| Mississippi | 4 lbs. 4 oz. | Arkabutla Reservoir | 3/19/1991 |
| Missouri | 5.0 lbs. | Private lake | 4/21/2006 |
| Montana * | 3.13 lbs. | Tongue River Reservoir | 1973 |
| Nebraska | 4 lbs. 8 oz. | Farm pond | 6/15/2003 |

## Black Crappie

| State | Weight | Place | Date |
|---|---|---|---|
| Nevada | 3 lbs. 2 oz. | Lake Mead | 4/23/1976 |
| New Hampshire | 2 lbs. 12.8 oz. | Bellamy Reservoir | 2/9/2000 |
| New Jersey | 4 lbs. 8 oz. | Pompton Lake | 1996 |
| New Mexico | 4 lbs. 9 oz. | Black River | 3/2/1983 |
| New York | 3 lbs. 12 oz. | Duck Lake | 4/17/1998 |
| North Carolina | 4 lbs. 15 oz. | Asheboro City Lake #4 | 4/27/1980 |
| North Dakota * | 3 lbs. 4 oz. | Lake Oahe | 2/7/1998 |
| Ohio | 4 lbs. 8 oz. | Private lake | 5/24/1981 |
| Oklahoma | 4 lbs. 10 oz. | Private pond | 5/1/1974 |
| Oregon | 4 lbs. 6.1 oz. | Pond Corvallis | 1995 |
| Pennsylvania * | 4 lbs. 2.88 oz. | Hammond Lake | 2000 |
| Rhode Island | 3 lbs. 0 oz. | Watchaug Pond | 7/1976 |
| South Carolina | 5 lbs. 0 oz. | Lake Moultrie | 1957 |
| South Dakota | 3 lbs. 9 oz. | SDSU pond | 5/27/2004 |
| Tennessee | 4 lbs. 4 oz. | Browns Creek Lake | 3/23/1985 |
| Texas | 3 lbs. 9.2 oz. | Lake Fork | 4/27/2003 |
| Utah | 3 lbs. 5 oz. | Lake Powell | 2009 |
| Vermont | 2 lbs. 7.52 oz. | Lake Champlain | 1999 |
| Virginia * | 4 lbs. 10 oz. | Private pond | 4/24/1994 |
| Washington | 4 lbs. 5 oz. | Lake Washington | 5/1/1956 |
| West Virginia * | 4.05 lbs. | Meathouse Fork | 1971 |
| Wisconsin | 4 lbs. 8 oz. | Gile Flowage | 8/12/1967 |
| Wyoming | 2 lbs. 5.44 oz. | Boysen Reservoir | 1997 |

## Chapter 2

# The Right Stuff
# Simplicity Vs. Fully Equipped

Way back in our college days, three wooden pegs above the door of Professor Posey's enclosed back porch cradled his fully-assembled 8-foot split bamboo fly rod with its reel affixed. Adjacent to the door was a built-in cabinet which displayed a small leather billfold containing leaders, tippet, and a vest pocket-sized tin box full of flies. Each item was essential to every fishing trip and no deviation was ever needed. The old professor's passion for fly-fishing was well known around campus and his simplistic approach never changed.

Most other fly-fishers in our acquaintance achieve the same blissful feelings with varying degrees of added paraphernalia. Some of us even overburden ourselves with numerous accessories that, when needed, can't even be located within our burgeoning vests or overstuffed boat bags. And yet we are as enthralled by fly-fishing as our more simplistic brethren. Unlike Professor Posey we confess to fitting somewhere into the upper echelon of the latter category.

Fly-fishing is wonderful in that respect because we all get to choose our own degree of sophistication and apply our own set of limits. As a result the sport is comprised of an interesting mosaic of individuals each dedicated to the concept of attracting and capturing fish through the use of a long and limber fly rod. All other aspects of fly-fishing are negotiable lying somewhere between pragmatism and the perceived ideal.

And so it is with the deepest respect for whatever definition of fly-fishing you've chosen that we offer the following discussion of equipment with the assurance that some will choose to eliminate some of the items.

Fly rods are designed to cast a specific line weight, ranging from very light through extremely heavy. This wide variance is expressed through a number system from 0-weight to 15-weight. For crappie fishing we recommend 3-weights through 7-weights. It's important to remember that line weight should be matched to the size, weight, and wind-resistance of the flies to be

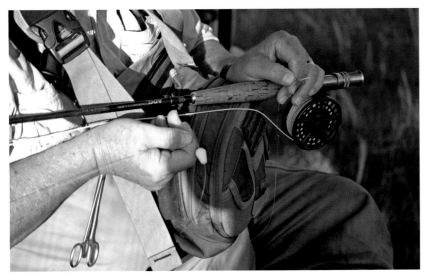

*All the fly-fisher needs for this trip is a single-action reel with floating line, waders, tackle pack, and a strike indicator.*

cast, not the size of the fish. There is a remarkable array of fly rod choices available today which includes the choice of material for the rod, rod length, types of ferrules and guides, type of reel seat, and action built into the rod. Many different manufacturers combine these choices into rods with functional and cosmetic differences to earn shares of a very complex market. Most fly rods today are made from graphite; some are supplemented by boron or titanium. These rods tend to be substantially lighter than other choices of materials and can be purchased in a wide range of prices and quality. A less expensive graphite rod isn't always inferior to a pricier model because cosmetic additions can escalate cost considerably. Many traditionalists choose to fish with classic bamboo rods, which offer an extraordinarily smooth cast but a lofty price tag and a heavier feel than graphite. Still others choose the fiberglass rods that dominated the market in the 1950's, 60's, and 70's. These rods are generally less expensive than either of the others and, again, are heavier than the other choices. All of these rod materials are perfectly capable of providing the fly-caster with a quality fly rod; the choice is simply a matter of preference and personal budget considerations.

Fly-rod length is primarily determined by the type of fishing you intend to do. Shorter rods are more adaptable to tight fishing quarters where overhead tree limbs and heavy bankside brush is a problem, while longer rods offer the ability to backcast over shoreline weeds and are superior when casting from a seated position because they keep the line off the water on the backcast. Rods of 7 feet to 9 feet easily handle most casting situations likely to be encountered by crappie enthusiasts.

Easily the most important fly-rod variable is its action. A slow rod loads more easily than a fast rod. By loading we refer to the flex of the rod on the backcast which enables the rod to throw or cast the line as the casting arc completes its forward movement. While a slow rod loads easily, the time it takes the line to straighten behind the caster is extended which makes the timing of when to begin the forward movement of the casting arm longer and therefore a bit more complex. What varying degree of slow vs. fast is best? That is personal preference that relates to your natural casting stroke, as well as to your experience in fly-casting. The more expert the caster the more easily he/ she will be able to adapt to either extreme quickly and easily. This is precisely why a fly rod should only be purchased after it's been tested. Two other aspects of the purchase are worthy of consideration. First, when you go to a fly shop with the intent of purchasing a new rod carry with you several flies that you intend to use with the rod. The hook points of each should be cut off. The customer cannot accurately assess a rod's suitability by casting line alone. The bulkier and heavier the fly, the more likely it is to alter the timing of the cast. Second, take a trusted, skilled caster along with you to observe your casts. That person will be able to see the rod action which best suits your casting stroke.

The complete crappie fly-fisher will, over the course of a season, cast many different flies. Some insect imitations are mere wisps of feathers without significant weight while other flies may be bulky and of considerable heft as flies go. For that reason the ideal rod arsenal would be a selection of rods ranging from 3-weight through 7-weight. If your budget requires but one rod a good choice would be a 6-weight. It would be able to deliver those small insect patterns, as well as cast some relatively heavy flies capable of reaching suspended crappies that might be located in 20 feet of water. Choosing the right fly rod is largely responsible for the angler's satisfaction with the casting process, and if an unwise choice is made by a beginner it could cause a loss of interest. When carefully selected and well cared for the fly rod can provide a lifetime of enjoyment.

## Reels

There are some who believe that fly reels should be very simple affairs because they mostly serve as line storage. In their opinions reels can be very inexpensive.

For crappie fly-fishers this is basically true; reels are a place to conserve on expenses for the budget conscious, but there are other considerations that must be taken into account.

Reels need to have enough spool capacity to accommodate backing. While crappies rarely run for distant cover, backing helps fill the spool so that more line can be recovered with each spool revolution. Backing also helps dry the line which prevents it from forming tight curls that inhibit casting. Fly-fishers need reels that satisfy five criteria: 1. Reels should be lightweight so as not to tire the all-day caster. 2. They should have enough capacity to accommodate at least 30 yards of backing. 3. Reels should enable the fly-fisher to change spools quickly and easily. 4. They should have good drag systems that are smooth and easily adjustable. 5. They should have an exposed reel rim that can be "palmed" when necessary to allow a big fish to take line and instantly brake a run when the fish must be kept away from heavy cover. While today's market is composed mostly of single-action reels there is another type, multiplying. Multiplying reels afford the advantage of recovering loose coils of line quickly but they are heavier than single-action reels and generally more expensive.

Single-action reels are easily the most popular because they offer all the features we've advocated without being too heavy or too complicated. There are lots of companies manufacturing fly reels today that offer the angler good choices from very inexpensive to high dollar. The differences are largely construction materials, design, and drag system. Reels that are fully machined from aerospace aluminum and have more technologically advanced drag systems are more expensive, grant lifetime guarantees and decades of trouble -free, hard use. For the serious-minded fly-fisher who fishes regularly they're a good investment. Most companies that manufacture high-quality reels offer superb craftsmanship with direct-drive and anti-reverse options on some models. When purchasing a fly reel the best advice is to buy the best you can reasonably afford and take care of it.

## Spare Spools

Year-around crappie fly-fishers must be able to present their flies in shallow water, at mid-depth, and over deep water. This would suggest the need for spare spools filled with different lines. When the fish are located in the shallows a spool of floating line works fine, but when they are in a brush pile at 12 feet a sink-tip, intermediate or even full-sinking line might be required. If the crappies

*Bank-stalking provides simplicity and plenty*
*of access to most crappie waters.*

are located just off the bottom in 20 feet of water, then perhaps the best approach is 25 feet of monofilament. Of course not all rods and, therefore, their reels are candidates for multiple spare spools. Three- and four-weights might serve best with just a single spool of floating line. Five- and 6-weights might use three spools containing floating, sink-tip, and lengthy monofilament lines and when the 7-weight is used as a deep-water tool with weighted flies it may only need a spool of monofilament line. For the one-rod angler three spools would be recommended. Spools are of course much less expensive than buying separate reels. Those who might consider using but one spool and one line should realize that it's as self-limiting as filling your fly box only with surface flies. There will simply be too many times when more options are needed to catch fish.

## Backing and Lines

For backing, 30-pound-test Dacron does the job nicely. Most reels require at least a hundred yards to fill the spool so that fly lines can be recovered using fewer turns. It's a mistake to mount backing, then change fly lines several times without checking to confirm the backing is in good shape and its knots are secure.

Fly-line quality should not be compromised to save on cost. It is the line that's cast. Cheap lines or those that are poorly matched to the rod's weight are a constant aggravation to the caster and inhibit good presentation.

Poorly chosen line is probably responsible for more beginners quitting the sport than any other single reason. Unfortunately, they were unable to discover the pure joy of effortless casting.

Modern fly lines need very little attention. They might accumulate dried moss and dirt, but nonabrasive soap and water or fly-line cleanser applied occasionally will keep them performing well. Avoid contact with anything that can cut or abrade the line and do not allow them to be stored in sunlight. Excessive heat and ultraviolet light will damage line. With a minimum of care a good fly line will last through several seasons. Lines should pass through the guides with little friction, which increases line speed and promotes accuracy.

Start with a weight-forward floating line of good quality. Some prefer light-colored or even fluorescent lines simply because they are easier to see. This choice enables the fisherman to detect strikes more easily and to see the line in the casting process. Both are helpful in learning and improving fly line control.

Sink-tip fly lines are rated in inches per second (i.p.s.). Sink-tip lines are rated as "slow" sinking, some at 1.5 i.p.s., and increase to 4 i.p.s. while full-sinking lines sink rates vary from 1 to 10 i.p.s. We prefer two full-sinking lines, one rated for 2 i.p.s. and another rated at 6 i.p.s. for crappie fishing. The first enables a streamer to be stripped just under the surface while the latter allows us to fish mid-depths for suspended crappies while allowing flies to get deep quickly.

Many modern lines come with a built-in front end loop. They're handy, but in the absence of factory-made loops, we employ a nail knot to secure the line to a piece of heavy monofilament that we finished in a perfection loop with a drop or two of head cement on each knot. This arrangement allows the knotted section to slip through the guides easily when necessary while securing the leader to the line in a manner that makes it readily interchangeable.

## The "Half Roll, Open Loop Cast"

Casting a sink-tip or full-sinking line is more difficult only because its submerged section is harder to pick up from the water. Traditionally fly-casters have stripped all but a few feet of these lines from the water before the pickup. As a result, several false casts are necessary before the line can be returned to the fish zone. It's hard work and wastes lots of time and motion, but casting sinking line is really quite simple. Rather than stripping in most of the line, simply lift the rod tip at a slight angle away from your body (the

position for beginning a roll cast). This action brings the fly line toward the surface regardless of how slowly it's performed. As the slack line drops from your rod tip in an arc beside you, punch your rod tip forward quickly with a roll-cast motion. Allow the line to straighten in front of you at eye level then pull briskly into a backcast. When the line straightens behind you bring your casting arm forward slowly to throw an open loop cast. You'll be able to shoot line efficiently and with a bit of practice will quickly learn the length of line you can leave in the water before beginning the cast.

## Leaders and Tippets

Some fly-fishers we've known brag that they can nurse a leader through an entire season. Okay, but to what end? This is another poor place to try to economize because the leader provides the final link between the line and the fly that the fly-fisher uses to fool the fish. If the fly appears unnaturally, it will almost certainly be rejected. Repeatedly tying on new tippet seems foolhardy when leaders are the angler's most inexpensive piece of essential equipment.

Leaders are highly adaptable tools that need to be matched to the fishing situation. They need to be as short as three to six feet on sinking lines and 7-1/2 to 12 feet on floating lines. Knotless leaders are best for most crappie waters because knots pick up moss, grass, weeds, and silt. The leader's tip needs to be stiff enough to keep the fly from hinging on the cast. The leader must turn over the fly efficiently yet withstand the abrasiveness of the targeted cover.

It can be helpful to select tippet material made by the same manufacturer as the leader to ensure the knots used to join them hold. Use as light a tippet as you can, especially in clear water, while maintaining the ability to deliver the chosen fly. Tippets from 5X to 2X generally will cover all the needs of crappie fly-fishers.

## Weighting and Floatant

When relying on casting to present the fly we've avoided using split shot because it can weaken the leader. Even BB-sized lead weights can cause hinging on the cast. When using a long length of monofilament with a strike indicator it is often necessary to use split shot to get the fly to the fish zone quickly. In that situation the cast has been forsaken and either becomes a lob or a toss with a vertical fishing presentation. We carry a small box of split shot in assorted sizes.

During the pre-spawn period in some waters crappies build their nests in very shallow water and will on occasion strike a surface fly. For that situation it's good to carry a small container of floatant to use with dry-fly patterns such as Elk Hair Caddis or Humpys.

## Hook Guards, Strike Indicators, and Slip Bobbers

Keeping flies from hanging up in the brush preferred by crappies can be a challenge. There is a large array of weedguard choices that use monofilament or wire but there are times the "take" of the fish is so soft that the weed-guard-rigged fly is rejected. It's also possible for a strand of mono on a weighted fly to be brushed aside by a limb or stump and the fly hangs up anyway. Fortunately there's a good alternative available. The product is called Stick-Guard. It's a short length of clear, soft plastic made of the same material that's used for rubber worms. The guard is flattened and slotted on one end. By slipping the hook eye of the fly through the slit, then embedding the blunted opposite end into the hook point the fly will be weedless and less likely to be rejected. They are inexpensive and although we've yet to find them in fly-fishing shops, we have found them in conventional-tackle stores. Keep in mind that these guards add a little weight to the flies.

Another option for presenting flies over the tops of brush, stumps, or weed beds is using a strike indicator set at the desired depth. This limits the use of weighted flies to the size and buoyancy of the strike indicator. A bit of experimentation will help you regulate size and weight. In general we use this system to present insect imitations with unweighted flies like soft hackles or lightly-weighted flies such as Woolly Worms.

## Hook Disgorger

Sometimes it's necessary to gently remove a deeply taken fly. Rather than risk injury to the fish, a good pair of surgical forceps not only handles this problem adequately, but can also serve as a debarbing tool when that task has been omitted at the tying vise.

## Lake Maps

If you are fishing a large body of water for which lake maps exist they will prove to be a good investment. The map should have the depth contours marked and if they also indicate the location of brush piles and other structural features, so much the better. The map can also show you the location of the confined open

## Diagram 2-A. Pond Fishing Locations (Self Mapping Examples)

**A.** Intermittant Inlet Creek

**B.** Dock

**C.** Deadfall

**D.** Silt Pile

**E.** Silt Pile/Mechanical Spillway

**F.** Standing Timber

**G.** Stump Patch

**H.** Rock Pile

**I.** Confined Open Water

**J.** Weed bed/Lilly Pads

**K.** Coontail Weed Bed

**L.** Overhanging Brush

water referred to in Chapter 1. For small lakes and ponds it's helpful to make your own maps. However crudely they are drawn, they help tremendously in locating crappies as the season progresses and aid in focusing on fish-holding areas. (See Diagram 2-A). These are the types of areas to mark on your own small-water maps. Notice that all areas, with possible exceptions of the rock pile (H) and the standing timber (F), can be effectively fished by the shore-bound angler. Most of the other locations enable presentations from several different positions. A float tube or small boat offers infinite presentation possibilities. Labeling each potential hot spot with letters or numbers, as the diagram shows, will enable the anglers to quickly refer to areas where fish are caught in specific weather patterns and to understand seasonal locations. The ability to identify possible fish locations in advance can be helpful.

## Lanterns and Floating Lights

Night fishing can be very productive for crappies but this is often a vertical jigging operation that requires strike indicators or slip bobbers and, of course, a lighting system. By placing aluminum foil on the backside of a standard camping lantern the light is forced onto the water's surface in front of your fishing location. The light attracts insects, which in turn attracts minnows and other small fish, which attracts the crappie population. Suspending a light-reflecting minnow imitation below the layer of insects and minnows is usually successful.

Another option to achieve the same result is purchasing a floating light which focuses the light into the water. These lights need a battery power source; a lawnmower battery preforms the task admirably as well as inexpensively.

## The Great Lantern Heist

Many years ago we joined another couple for a week-long houseboat excursion on Tennessee's famed Dale Hollow Reservoir. We moved about the massive lake in the houseboat camping in a different location every night while fishing from a 14-foot jon boat powered with a 10-horse motor. After four days of poor fishing we decided to take the small boat into a marina with a restaurant for dinner and seek some sage advice concerning the fishing. After a good, hot meal we met the elderly owner named "Jessie" on the porch of the establishment. He acknowledged that fishing had been slow but told us that limits of slab crappies could be caught by night fishing with lanterns. We were definitely interested of course, but didn't have any lanterns. The helpful marina owner had the solution. He just happened to have a couple of lanterns in his shed on the dock and he'd be happy to rent them to us for the very reasonable price of $3.00 apiece per night.

"Great! We'll take them," we chorused.

As we picked up the lanterns and began walking toward our boat the old gentleman called after us, "Will y'all be a-needin' any mantles for them lanterns?"

Well . . . yes, of course we would. They were offered at a mere $2.00 per lantern per night which we paid and, again, turned to depart.

"How 'bout fuel? Y'all got any fuel?"

Nope, but a can was added to our bill for $5.00. Cautiously, we asked, "Is that all we need?"

"Well," drawled the old entrepreneur, "You could probably use some aluminum foil which I have right here and will only cost a dollar."

Jessie's parceled-out lanterns ended up costing us a total of $36.00, which at the time would have been enough to buy three brand-new lanterns. Could it be that Jessie James was alive and well? We did catch a lot of big crappies.

## Vests, Boat Bags, and Tackle Packs

When fishing from a boat or canoe we prefer to use a boat bag capable of carrying a number of fly boxes and leaders, tippet material, and all the paraphernalia we might need. However, if wade fishing is the assignment, there are several viable options. Traditionalists will want to use vests. They hold lots of tackle and allow the security of knowing that we'll usually have what we need. They can be heavy however, and on hot summer days, vests can feel suffocating. Traveling light is a good plan for hot-weather wading and there are a variety of tackle packs that have become standard for lots of anglers. The real issue depends on how much gear you feel you need to carry with you.

## Waders, Boots, and Gravel Guards

Those who fish streams or fish from a float tube, especially during periods when the water is cool, will need waders. We prefer lightweight breathable stocking-foot chest waders. For us they are the most comfortable and we can use them through the colder months by layering our clothing.

Stocking-foot models allow the use of the boots alone while wet wading during the warmest part of the year. Gravel that finds its way over boot tops is terribly uncomfortable and can wear holes in stocking feet quickly. Gravel guards are an inexpensive solution to the problem, whether wearing waders or wading wet. Waders often come with gravel guards attached, so the purchase of a separate pair may be unnecessary.

## Float Tubes

Even as youngsters we recognized the advantage of reaching waters other anglers couldn't fish. Using an old car tire inner tube with a board across the middle as a seat and a paddle for propulsion gave us that access, but clearly the apparatus lacked comfort and style. In the early seventies, we purchased a molded plastic model. It was a bit heavy and cumbersome to carry but it was a marvelous improvement. Today's inflatable, non-rotting models incorporate comfortable seats, lots of storage space, backrests, even casting aprons to keep loose fly line from dangling into the water, entangling feet and fins. Most have tape-measure markings along the apron for measuring fish.

*In ponds, float tubes enable easy access to the best crappie hangouts.*

*Bass boats offer comfort, stable casting platforms,*
*and great range for covering big waters.*

## Canoes and Kayaks

Canoes and kayaks are comparatively lightweight and can be car-topped or trailered, then portaged to waters without improved boat ramps. This affords fly-casters the opportunity to fish waters that are inaccessible to many. On the other hand, if you have difficulty casting from a seated position without rocking back and forth, they would not be the best fishing craft for you.

## Crappie Boats

Fishermen have a wider selection of boats available to them now than ever before. The most coveted boat style is a bass boat. With its exceptionally stable casting platform it seems perfect for the fly-caster but there are many exposed knobs and projections to catch and entangle fly line. Virtually all could be recessed or eliminated but certainly every high-tech gadget that has been incorporated into the design of these big-lake monsters is as useful to the fly-rod-wielding crappie angler as the ardent basser. Ordinary aluminum boats may be inexpensively customized by adding plywood flooring, carpeting, and padded swivel seats.

Float tubes, canoes, kayaks, small prams, and luxurious bass boats can all be equipped with electric trolling motors, anchoring systems, locators, temperature gauges, and measuring rulers for quickly determining legal length for keepers. An anchoring system may not be worth the investment if you mostly fish large lakes with areas of water too deep to keep an anchor from reaching the bottom. Locators, on the other hand are very useful to the crappie angler both in locating brush piles as well as finding suspended fish in confined open-water areas.

Temperature gauges that only give surface readings are not particularly helpful; but those that are capable of being lowered to various depths and, at the push of a button, give a digital readout of the temperature at a particular depth can be invaluable.

Now that we've come to know our quarry and have selected the necessary gear, let's go crappie fishing.

## Chapter 3

# The Crappie's Spring: The Great Migration

W inter's icy grip forces isolation on many warmwater enthusiasts. Long hours of televised entertainment soon melt into weeks, then months. Even time spent at the tying vise begins to weigh heavily upon the spirits of those too long prevented from the pursuit of gamefish. And then it happens.

A few warm days are followed by rumors that crappie are being caught. Excitement permeates the community as barber and coffee shop conversations chronicle the local catch. A massive double migration explodes with activity as crappies invade the shallows in a frantic search for food and an army of anglers, overwhelmed by their desire to wet a line, migrate to their favorite waters. This rite of spring for both crappies and anglers begins each year in the deep South as waters first begin to warm, and like a giant tidal wave moves ever northward until it encompasses the entirety of the crappie's range.

As one of the earliest warmwater gamefish to spawn, the crappie's initial foray into thin waters marks the first opportunity for fishermen to encounter shallow-feeding fish. After months of inactivity, feeling the throb of life on their rods grants a thirst-quenching feeling that prompts a need to experience it again and again. Throughout the spring season crappies oblige anglers as millions are caught.

Just knowing that crappies prefer thick entanglements and sometimes spend their time schooled in confined open areas is not enough. For fishing success we need to predict within narrow limits where the largest concentrations of fish will be located at any given time. To do this we must understand the special needs of crappies during the spring season, how and why they react to their environments, and how daily weather changes affect their movements and behaviors.

As a captive of an enclosed environment the crappie's world is governed, among other variables, by water temperatures so an exact date for the crappies' spring is subject to the whims of nature, not specified by a calendar, nor does it arrive at the same time in all locations. In fact, if you were to fish your

*Early spring crappies migrate to the shallows because minnows and shad have located there. Use weighted streamers for good results.*

way north from Florida into the southern portion of the Canadian Provinces targeting only the prespawn it would be a journey that easily could consume four months. Anglers in Florida might be fishing summer conditions while those in the extreme northern areas might still be waiting for ice-out. But it is reasonable to make some general observations about seasonal fish movements based on water temperatures.

If the water temperature is in the mid-60-degree range, whether we are talking about Lake Okeechobee, Florida or Pelican Lake, Minnesota, the crappies will be involved in the spawning process. Much like their human counterparts, not all crappies respond to the same stimuli in the same way, at the same time. Some may get an early start while others begin to spawn when the temperature gauge says they should be in summer quarters. Our objective is to discover what most of the crappies are doing at a given time, thereby enabling us to maximize our catches.

This initial surge into the shallows is not related to spawning. The crappies simply follow their target prey species into the shallows. Warmer waters increase their metabolism, which heightens their need to feed. Although they are aggressive feeders at this time they are also more skittish than usual as the deep environments of winter are forsaken for thin waters. Crappies are easier to catch in the spring than at any other time but are also very intolerant of sloppy casts, boat noises, and other disturbances.

### Early Spring

This is a period of transition for the crappies from winter's lethargy to a cool-water environment. This transition is most easily accomplished in periods of stable weather. As warm, calm days continue the crappies spend an increasing amount of time feeding in the shallows. Often anglers think of fishing as an early morning, late evening event, but in early spring the fish will be most active when sunshine finds the water. Mid- to late afternoon when the water is warmest is clearly best. Fly-fishers can also tilt the odds in their favor by targeting coves and bays with dark bottoms. This is because the dark color absorbs more of the sun's warmth thereby being a few degrees warmer than other areas. Just a couple degrees of water temperature at this time will attract many hungry crappies, while a similar nearby cove with a lighter-colored bottom may have none or very few.

*If small flies don't produce strikes try dropping weighted flies into the crappies' nests.*

Springtime, particularly the earliest portion, is seldom a time of stable weather. Most years cold fronts move through in rapid succession. Each occurrence interrupts the shallow feeding activity of the crappies and they retreat to deeper water. During the summer season it's the post cold-front conditions (cloudless, bright sunshine) that cause shallow feeders to abandon thin water, but that's not the case in early spring. It's not the sun's glare that drives crappies deeper; it's the cooling of the water itself. Once again, a degree or two becomes critical in determining the location of the fish. But if the crappies have moved out of the shallows and into deeper water, where specifically will they be located and can they be targeted and caught there? The answer is that they will move to locations we call "staging areas." In both reservoirs and natural lakes staging areas are found at the first breakline and, depending upon the severity of the cold front, will locate either in heavy brush or along emerging weed growth. The first breakline is easily recognized on natural lakes because it marks the depth beyond which weed growth is possible because sunlight penetration cannot reach the lake's floor. Crappies will retreat to this weedline and wait for more favorable and stable conditions to return to the shallows. Even when the water is not warm enough to promote weed growth, these retreating crappies will relate to dead weeds. Most likely they will suspend in relation to the deep edge of these decaying weeds. In reservoirs, rapid water fluctuations often eliminate weed growth so brush located at the first drop-off or breakline becomes the staging area. These staging-area crappies are still hungry and can be caught, but the tactics must change from shallow-shoreline casting to a deeper-water presentation. Northern natural lakes may warm differently from one another. Shallow, weedy lakes with silt bottoms warm quickly enough that they can be fished successfully while a nearby deep, rocky body of water may still have shoreline ice. On reservoirs the timing of shallow runs is related to the size of the body of water. A pond of 15 acres will provide shallow fishing much earlier than a nearby reservoir of many thousands of acres. It's not uncommon for crappies to suspend near their staging areas, but usually this will be in direct relationship to the staging area's structure.

Staging areas can sometimes be determined by a visual reconnaissance of the spawning area. By knowing where crappies spawn within a given cove or on a certain flat the angler can survey the surrounding topography. Generally, a spawning area will extend from a low-lying shoreline to deeper water in areas of low-lying terrain. If the bank begins to get steeper nearby and if there is other structure such as a brush pile, weedline, or boat dock in conjunction with the drop off into deeper water, it certainly is worth exploring. Most often the staging area will be in close proximity to the spawning site. If the cold front is especially severe and colder weather persists for several days, the crappie are more likely to move further away from the shallows, even returning to their cold-water hangouts.

When crappies are feeding on shallow flats they are there to prey upon a shad or minnow population they've followed there. Fly selection and presentation are simple in this situation. Any streamer pattern that replicates the size and color of the natural served on a weight-forward line with a leader and tippet chosen to turn the fly over efficiently will furnish good action. During early spring, with water temperatures in the 40's, the crappie's metabolism is still a bit slow, so action may be steady but hardly at prespawn pace. Leaders of 9 feet may be necessary to get those streamers to the three- to five-foot depths the fish may be utilizing. Several days of stable weather will push the fish and their prey into shallow weedlines and the backs of coves. Adjust the weight and speed of your retrieve to the depth of the fish. In just a few feet of water use lightly weighted streamers that push a bit of water and retrieve them with erratic strips. If the fish are holding at three to five feet use a heavier version of the same streamer and count the fly down by mentally counting "one-thousand-one, one-thousand-two," etc. to get your fly to the right depth. Your counting speed may vary from the next angler's but it doesn't matter as long as you know the sink rate of your fly. If you make fish contact at a count of eight, for example, you know that you should return to that depth on succeeding casts.

Fishing the staging areas requires sink-tip or full-sinking line, flies with a bit of weight, a short leader of three to six feet to prevent the fly from bowing back toward the surface, and the countdown method previously described. The fish that have retreated from the shallows will be willing feeders but are less aggressive and less willing to chase their meals. Long casts are necessary in fishing the 10- to 15-foot depths these fish may occupy. This means either leaving slack line directly over the target to allow the fly to descend straight into the depths or casting a tight line well past the target to allow the fly to swing toward the target as it drops through the water. Each strip should be followed by a pause to allow the fly to settle to its original depth. This is a challenging presentation but the angler can derive great satisfaction from it. A bit of practice will enhance success.

### Prespawn (50's to Low 60's)

As water temperatures reach the 50-degree range, crappies move into prespawn behavior. Their objective at this time is not to feed, but to procreate. This doesn't mean they won't bite. Quite the contrary, their territorial instincts at this time bring an aggressive, even combative attitude that's much to the angler's advantage. While not specifically feeding, male crappies are building nests and are intent upon driving any intruders away.

Nest-builders are seeking waters that are warmer than the surrounding area, a semi-soft bottom, and some cover in the form of weeds or brush. Button Bush, one of the most common emergent brush species in the mid-South, provides excellent cover for shallow spawning sites but their wood branches require the use of weedguards. On larger bodies of water see if a warm southern breeze blows these warmer waters toward the north shore. The ideal crappie spawning cove is situated to receive these warming breezes. The back of the cove will be at the northern end where the sun is able to shine for the longest period of the day. Sunshine has further importance because it contributes abundant plankton as a food source for crappie hatchlings. The cove's north shoreline may also furnish some protection from cold fronts' chilly north winds. Wind can be difficult for fly-fishers to contend with because it affects casting accuracy, boat control, and even the ability to hold an anchored position. It can cause wave action across the spawning area, which may cause male nest-builders to abandon the area and retreat to deeper water.

Coves with creeks that enter at their narrow ends support weed growth or hold wood deadfalls that often have ideal spawning areas. These creeks bring warmer water into the cove and the movement of the water to add oxygen as well. These very shallow creek-mouth areas can provide some of the best and fastest fishing of the entire year, but great care must be taken to avoid startling the crappies. Hang-ups can send the fish scurrying for deeper water. Some hang-ups are inevitable, of course, but when they occur simply rest the area for 15 to 20 minutes before returning to resume casting. Small streamers and jig-type flies that can be fished slowly can be the ticket to success. If stickups, brush or weeds pose hang-up problems be prepared to use a weedguard. If small flies fail to produce good action try dropping a weighted fly right into the nests. Remember these male pre-spawners are very territorial but not actively feeding.

As the prespawn period progresses the fish become increasingly aggressive, which delivers the easiest fishing of the entire year. At times virtually any cast that hits the water in these shallow areas can bring a lusty strike, but clearly attention to detail will bring even more sustained action. Casts that produce a heavy splashdown should be avoided and noisy approaches may spook the entire area. Approach the shallows cautiously. If using a boat, cut the motor at least 50 yards from the intended fishing area and move quietly into position. If the sun is at your back be careful not to cast shadows across the shallow flat. Bank fishermen, even on small waters such as ponds, canals or small streams, need also to be conscious of the positions of their shadows. It may be necessary to crouch or kneel to cast to these sensitive shallow areas. These male fish are distracted by their spawning urges to be sure, but still quite intolerant of these fish-scattering gaffs.

While the nest-building process continues in the shallows, females are located in adjacent deeper water awaiting development of their eggs and nature's call to begin their spawning activities. While still staging, females continue feeding and once located can be caught with the presentations discussed previously in relation to the staging area. (See Diagram 3-A and 3-B). Note that the staging areas in both natural lakes and reservoirs may be located a considerable distance from the spawning flat or in close proximity depending on what is available. In targeting the female population anglers must decide if this is wise. While one or even several anglers may not affect the success of the spawn by removing egg-laden females, many might. The ethics of this issue may depend on the targeted population. We prefer to return egg-bearing females to the water gently and quickly, and if any fish are kept, take only males during this sensitive prespawn period. Check slot limits on public waters and owner recommendations on private waters.

Riverine crappie populations seek the quiet backwaters devoid of current. This may be an oxbow lake connected to a large river or a small pocket of protected water away from the stream's main flow. (See Diagram 3-C). Often these areas have silted or sandy bottoms with abundant weed growth and brush or deadfalls that have washed into the area.

Small ponds warm more quickly than other bodies of water, so they furnish anglers with their first opportunity for shallow fishing. On most ponds the deepest water is found near the dam. The shallows are often located where an intermittent creek enters the pond. Bank-stalkers should approach the area cautiously to avoid scaring the crappies and begin by fishing adjacent deeper areas. Any brush pile, deadfall or weedline remnants should be thoroughly fished.

Once again weather plays a critical role in the rise of water temperatures toward the 60-degree mark and therefore the process of the spawn. Cold fronts often force males off the spawning grounds and back to the staging area. It's not uncommon for several movements to the shallows, then back to the first breakline to occur. If bad weather persists for too long it can even threaten the spawn and cause the ripened females to drop their eggs, thus aborting the spawn altogether.

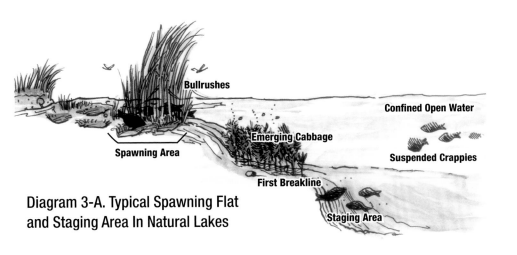

**Bullrushes**

**Confined Open Water**

**Emerging Cabbage**

**Spawning Area**

**Suspended Crappies**

**First Breakline**

## Diagram 3-A. Typical Spawning Flat and Staging Area In Natural Lakes

**Staging Area**

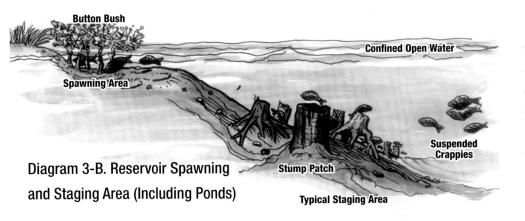

**Button Bush**

**Confined Open Water**

**Spawning Area**

**Suspended Crappies**

## Diagram 3-B. Reservoir Spawning and Staging Area (Including Ponds)

**Stump Patch**

**Typical Staging Area**

## The Spawn (Low to Mid 60's)

As water temperatures on the shallow flats reach 60 degrees male crappies turn a darker color and become even more aggressive. Their defense against any intruder intensifies so they become easier to catch, but this angler's bonanza is relatively short-lived. When females begin to join the males in the nests, spawning occurs. During the actual spawning process females may drop some eggs in a male's nest, then return to the staging area briefly before returning to deposit eggs in other males' nests. This may occur several times before the females have dropped all their eggs. Older females with the most body mass carry the most eggs and visit the most nests, while first-time spawners may only spawn with a single male.

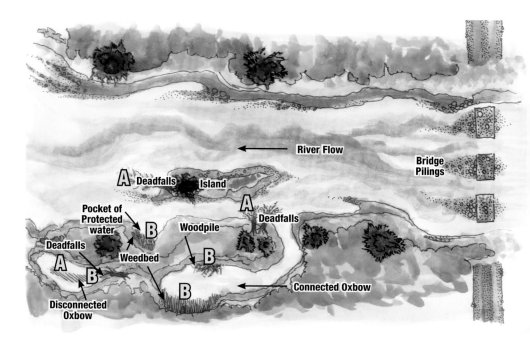

**Diagram 3-C. Typical Spawning and Staging Areas for Rivers and Oxbows**
**A.** Staging Areas
**B.** Spawning Sites

For the entire population to complete the spawning process may take several weeks. Throughout the nesting and rearing season the male crappie remains near the nest to guard the eggs, which hatch in a few days under ideal conditions. The male is extremely vulnerable during his protective period, and if a male is removed at this critical time his entire brood will be subjected to intense predation from bass, bluegills, and other fish. Once again we would encourage a catch-and-release policy for this sensitive time. It's important to note again that not all crappies spawn at the same time. Some will be ahead of schedule while others lag behind, so a portion of the population might be in prespawn while others will actively spawn, and perhaps others will experience post-spawn.

In waters that are dark or stained spawning will take place in water that's shallower than in clear water. Very darkened, shallow waters sometimes host nest-builders with their backs above the water line, but for most two feet is common. In very clear water where visibility extends to six feet for example, spawning may take place somewhere between seven feet and nine feet depending on bottom content and available weeds and brush.

# Big John and the Exploding Duck Blind

For 25 years Terry duck hunted with an affable giant who had a reputation for being unusually strong willed. Some would have described him as hot-tempered. Big John stood over 6 feet 2 inches tall and weighed a bit north of 300 pounds. It was no secret that he considered all the backwater lakes near town as his own private hunting preserve. He hunted where he pleased and no one ever disputed his choices. Together the two had built their duck blind and hunted in the north end of a large oxbow lake that backed up against a huge island which harbored numerous ponds and small lakes. Ducks flew out into the vast fields of grain to the east to feed and returned to the main lake or the island ponds to rest. It was a nearly perfect place in which to intercept wave after wave of mallards, pintails, and other ducks. Most days at least a few were called into Big John and Terry's decoys. But late in this particular season the waterfowl shifted their flight pattern to the south. Ducks could be seen traversing an area of the lake known as "the narrows."

After three days of inaction Big John had had enough. "We're movin'," he announced.

The hunters set up adjacent to the narrows in a club-owned blind to intercept the ducks' new flight path. Minutes after settling into the new area a pair of Mallard drakes banked over the willow-lined shore and careened into the decoys. A volley of shots dropped both. This would be a memorable evening.

In the distance the drone of a single small outboard motor became audible. Minutes later the skiff could be seen coming toward Big John and Terry. Fifty yards away a bearded man stood in the bow of the oncoming boat gesturing wildly and shouting obscenities amidst threats of violence against his "poachers." Big John was neither amused nor intimidated but picked up the two dozen decoys spread around the blind and without comment slowly motored into the narrow channel which led to the main lake where he opened the throttle and aimed the boat toward the landing. Still silent, Big John was red-faced mad and seething. Suddenly the boat swung into a U-turn and accelerated to top speed. While not surprised, Terry dreaded the confrontation he knew was ahead.

The boat sped through the narrow channel and into the pothole scattering decoys in its wake. From his perch in the boat's bow Terry could see the wide-eyed occupants of the blind scramble to their feet and leap in opposite directions into the icy waters. The boat's impact with the blind scattered broken willow branches, mud, and wooden blind flooring into the air in all directions.

Without losing speed Big John made another U-turn at the end of the slough, and just as much of the crash debris was landing on the water made another pass through the floating trash.

Back at the landing, a shaken, but unhurt Terry turned toward Big John whose demeanor had completely changed. A broad smile of satisfaction spread across his countenance and he spoke for the first time, "Sorry 'bout destroyin' that blind; I know it wuz yur crappie hotspot, but they'll rebuild."

The area had long been a spring crappie location because the willowed boat hide had been excavated by the hunters' coming and goings. The hole was perhaps a foot deeper than the surrounding silted bottom and the willow branch stickups served as protective structure. We had caught many large crappies from the area, but despite the blind being rebuilt we never returned to fish it again.

### The Post Spawn (Mid 60's to 70 Degrees)

As water temperatures reach the upper-60's females will begin to drift away from the shallows and enter nearby deeper water. For them this post-spawn period is a time of recovery from the rigors of the spawn. Females are usually scattered during the early post-spawn which may last depending upon the weather conditions for a couple of weeks. They aren't very active during this time but will feed if an easy meal is at hand. Since they're not concentrated they can be difficult to interest consistently.

Male crappies become protective parents after spawning. They stay near the nests to drive away any prospective predators, fan the nests with their tails to furnish the eggs with oxygen and remove any debris or silt that could cover and destroy the eggs. The dutiful parents remain on guard until the hatchlings are dispersed, which is a period of about a week if cold weather doesn't intervene. This is a time, as previously noted, when males are extremely vulnerable and should be left alone. While targeting females is more difficult it can be rewarding fishing. Often these fish are suspended in water from 5 to 15 feet depending on what's available to them. It should be noted that often suspended crappies are very specific about their depth. We've often encountered fish that are lying from 10-1/2 feet to 12-1/2 feet, as an example, and that were scattered over an area of approximately thirty square yards. Remember that the crappies' eyes are located so near the tops of their heads it encourages them to feed above their positions. In these situations one can easily see why good depth control on the presentation is necessary.

Trolling the edges of crappie pods, whether with a boat and motor, a kayak, canoe or float tube, can be effective if strict attention is paid to depth control. During this portion of the late post-spawn males and females are milling about in search of food. Concentrate your efforts along the deep sides of weedlines or near the first deeper structures if no weedlines are present. Post-spawn crappies in rivers move from the oxbow or inlet to areas in the flow that afford a current break. Search for nearby brush piles, deadfalls, the toe of islands or bridge pilings and fish them thoroughly. With these fish in a more aggressive, even chasing attitude trolling becomes the best option of presentation. A sink-tip line or slowly sinking full-sink line can afford success. The key, as with any trolling operation, is speed control. Usually it's best to make the first trolling runs at slow speeds, but this is an instance when speed can be increased to allow the angler to cover a larger area. If the lake has many docks within the spawning cove with immediate access to relatively deep water they may serve as staging areas. It's likely that not every dock in a row of docks will attract staging crappies. Pay attention to those closest to the spawning flats and those with other attractions like brush or weeds. Cast to the deepest portion of the dock pilings first and retrieve the fly very slowly at a variety of depths. Especially in full sunlight, cast as far back under the dock as possible. At times several crappies may be caught, and then suddenly they might turn off. When this happens, move to the next dock and rest the area where you had success for 15 to 20 minutes then return. Often the fish will have a renewed appetite.

As crappies suspend in post spawn it's usually not difficult to find them. First, look at the entrances to the spawning cove or bay, especially if the area qualifies as confined open water. This will almost certainly hold crappies. While the task of locating these suspended crappies is not difficult it becomes much easier with a locator. This is particularly true on large, deep lakes. As a very adaptable species crappies use what is available to them. If silt-bottomed spawning areas are the only places available to them, they will adapt to and use those areas. Chances are that the spawn will be less successful and consequently the crappie population is likely to be much less vibrant. If the body of water is relatively small, post-spawn crappie may be forced to retreat to the deepest water in the pond to suspend. In this situation, without a locator it really is a case of blind trial and error. As pointed out in Chapter 2, locators are adaptable to virtually any floatation device or watercraft. Fancier models can be expensive but finding one that identifies bottom features, weeds, brush, and fish as well as displaying the surface water temperature can be had for a relatively small price. If you have become frustrated trying to locate suspended fish and realize that you are basically confined to fishing the shallow flats or hoping for an accidental encounter with suspended fish you may be a good candidate for the purchase of a fish locator. Locator users need to learn all they can about their units. You should know how to adjust them and bring up the information you want and need. Start by reading all the information that comes with your unit then take it out and experiment until you are comfortable with its operation. Even though power boats enable the angler to roam around huge lakes and impoundments in search of fish they are not necessary to be successful. Locate a spawning cove, launch a canoe, kayak or float tube, and you can have the same access to fish as those big boats. These smaller crafts may even afford access to areas the bass boats can't reach and also enable a gentler approach to structure.

The shorebound angler is also able to access most of these same areas. If there is a lake map marked with placed brush piles, notice that almost every one of them is within casting distance of shore. Some will be where the terrain is too steep for standing or there is too little back-casting room, but there will be many that offer good access. By concentrating on fishing the brush and the nearby shallow spawning flats those that choose to fish from shore can be equally successful. For these anglers the best situation is locating several of these brushy areas within relatively close proximity to each other. If one area needs resteing or if a fly needs to be broken off, move to another area and return later. Cast all around the brush area and experiment with various depths and retrieves. Often a steadily stripped fly that is paused for a second, causing the fly to freefall, can be very effective.

As the post-spawn progresses crappies tend to move progressively deeper, which actually moves them into their summer haunts. By fishing regularly throughout the early spring and into the end of the post-spawn the angler will be able to stay on the fish, and in the process understand the progression of their movements and changing needs.

When the fry have dispersed, males rejoin the now recuperated female population at the first breakline to cruise the outsides of weedlines and locations near brush piles or deadfalls. Both sexes are searching for food and move along these deeper areas for meals. In the process they form large, distinct schools. When adult crappies abandon the spawning grounds altogether the post-spawn period has ended. Almost imperceptibly the crappie population slips into their summer residences and activities.

*Dams with mechanical spillways and riprap are
great places to begin a crappie fishing trip.*

*Chapter 4*

# Warmwater Crappies

There are two foolproof methods of determining that the crappie spawn is over and summer has arrived. First, the fish have disappeared from the shallow flats and second, fishermen are no longer pursuing them. Most anglers, especially fly-fishers, simply abandon crappie fishing during the summer months because they believe the fish have become more difficult to locate, and even when they are discovered fly presentations at the increased depths pose some problems. While there's no doubt that the fishing is more challenging there are some simple adaptations that enable fly-fishers to compete favorably with their conventional-tackle counterparts.

As warmer weather arrives crappies move from the first breakline in natural lakes or the closest deeper structure in reservoirs from the spawning coves to more main-lake deeper-water locations. This is very often the confined open water of a cove mouth. Unlike bass and bluegill populations they do not gravitate toward shallow weedlines or lily pad bays. Instead, they seek out either confined open water or deep structure like brush piles, deep weeds, rock piles or standing timber. This change of location usually takes place when water temperatures reach the lower 70's. This is a time when weedlines are growing, insects are hatching, and large schools of newly-hatched fry are visible. Feeding opportunities abound amid summer's abundance. In natural lakes crappies may suspend near the deep portion of weedlines to prey upon the smorgasbord it provides. In reservoirs they may utilize the edges of submerged rivers or creek channels while river residents leave the backwater shallows for the deeper edges of current to take up lies to feed on whatever the river's flow contributes.

The crappie population can be difficult to locate as they move toward these areas of abundance, but very soon a pattern emerges. The beginning couple of weeks of summer is a time of change and movement that settles into a time of plenty.

While referring primarily to deep-water locations we need to recognize that these situations dominate northern natural lakes and the mid-South's sprawling reservoirs, but there are many bodies of water that simply don't have truly deep water. In this situation crappies migrate from the shallow flats to the deepest water available for their summer homes. Our experience with these fisheries is that crappies tend to suspend at very specific depths and that during patterns of stable weather they will be spread horizontally over a large area. If the deepest water available is 14 feet, for example, in the center of a 200-acre lake summer crappie might suspend between 11 feet and 13 feet but will spread out over a couple of acres. It's important to note that the depths of crappie suspension in this example change in response to weather changes, sunlight penetration, water temperature, and available structure.

Many years ago we fished a similar lake that was quite old and heavily silted. It was owned by a country club that managed it for swimming and a variety of water sports to include paddle boats, canoes, and row boats. Most of the fishing was done by children with cane poles or grownups who tight-lined for catfish. Most of the crappie spawn took place along a big beach area consisting of trucked-in sand. Fishing during the spawn was easy and outstanding, but when it ended the fish just seemed to disappear. Finally, armed with one of the early flasher locator units, we set out to find them. At first we tried looking for submerged brush or weeds but found none. Siltation had in effect created a large fish bowl devoid of any defined physical features. From the shoreline the lake just grew progressively and gradually deeper into a trough 14 feet deep. With the deepest water found we triangulated using permanent shorebound structures so we could easily return and then scoured the area for fish. Instead of finding fish tightly grouped we found scattered fish within a very confined set of depths. Casting to the area seemed to be a waste of time. Although some were caught they were too few and far between. Eventually we determined that trolling this open-water area while paying strict attention to depth control brought the kind of success we sought. We further discovered that in this dark-water environment the crappies often suspended at depths of three to five feet over the 14-foot bottom. The depth of suspended crappie should be considered a daily variable. Certainly under stable weather conditions the fish are likely to remain in the same or similar positions, but the change may also be related to the movements of the available prey. It should also be noted that when using a locator it's a bad idea to try to isolate individual fish and cast to them. Instead, look for schools or pods of fish and note their distance horizontally and vertically from one another. As the angler searches an area for fish it is important to understand the relationship of the boat's speed to

Diagram 4-A.
Natural Lakes Summer Locations
**A.** Bullrushes
**B.** Cabbage
**C.** Suspended Crappies
**D.** Active Feeders Along Deep Edge
   of Weed Lilne and in Weed Pockets
**E.** First Breakline
**F.** Secondary Breakline
**G.** Cold Front Location

the distance between fish. If for example, you cruise at a moderate speed while running the locator, it may appear on the unit's screen that fish are tightly bunched, but when you look at the distance the boat has travelled you realize that they are quite widely scattered.  While we logically would think that trolling a streamer that replicates the size, shape, and color of crappies' natural prey is best, often the fish respond better to a jig-type fly with independently moving parts such as rubber legs or marabou. Especially in this early summer period smaller flies are usually most effective. This is because the size of the crappies' prey is also small. Sizes 8 and 10, lightly-weighted marabou jig flies can be successful. It's also important to match the color of your fly with the conditions. In dark waters, most especially on overcast days or early and late in the day, a black marabou fly may be most effective simply because it is more visible to the fish due to the stark silhouette it offers.

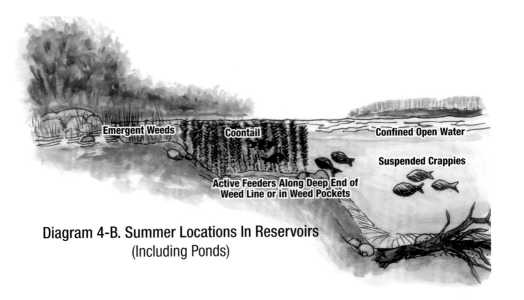

Emergent Weeds

Coontail

Confined Open Water

Suspended Crappies

Active Feeders Along Deep End of
Weed Line or in Weed Pockets

**Diagram 4-B. Summer Locations In Reservoirs**
**(Including Ponds)**

### The Summer Pattern

As water temperatures reach the mid-70's the other warmwater species have completed their spawn and clouds of fry are available to the crappie population for predation. In natural lakes the fish patrol the deep weedline while their reservoir-inhabiting cousins gorge themselves on young shad along the submerged creek channels. Fishing can be tremendous for anglers who are knowledgeable about the crappies' new locations. The crappies are ravenous, aggressive, and heavily schooled which prompts competitive feeding at a time when the lake is full of fry and insects. The lake and river environments are in full bloom. This is a productive period to pursue crappies, yet their movements seem to bewilder many of those that have pursued them successfully in the shallows during the spawn.

As crappies settle into their summer pattern they generally occupy the depths between 5 and 20 feet. One obvious aid in helping to determine their depth is the knowledge that they will be deeper in clear water and shallower in stained water. If deep weeds such as coontail exist, whether in reservoirs, ponds, natural lakes, or rivers the most active fish will be close to the edge of the weeds, and if the weeds are sparse, explore a bit into them. Inactive crappies will usually suspend in relation to the weeds. They will be located in open water outside the weeds from several feet to 20 yards or so. If the deep weed edges are not productive then follow the contours of the weedline at progressively greater distances. This can be done with a locator, of course, but trolling will also aid in the location process. (See Diagrams 4-A and 4-B.)

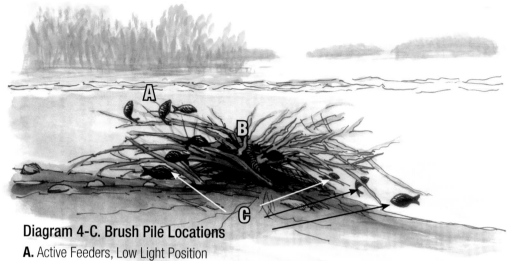

**Diagram 4-C. Brush Pile Locations**
**A.** Active Feeders, Low Light Position
**B.** Active Feeders, Located in Brush to Avoid Sunlight
**C.** Post Cold Front Locations

In many reservoirs weed cover is absent. In this case fly-fishers are looking at deep-water rock piles, standing timber, stump patches, manmade fish attractors, boat houses, docks, old duck blinds or brush piles. To the crappie fisherman brush piles can be both a blessing and a curse. They are a blessing because they so frequently hold crappies. They're a source of frustration because they contribute constant opportunities to hang-up your fly, and rest assured you will hang-up. When it becomes necessary to break off, the best advice is back off and rest the area for 15 to 20 minutes. You'll need to tie on a new fly anyway. (See Diagram 4-C). The active feeders in low-light positions are easy targets as long as depth control is maintained. The crappies located in the middle of the brush are challenging but very catchable. Those crappies located in the post cold-front position will bite but not chase a meal.

There are several ways to present flies to brush and they all involve utilizing a weed guard. First try casting or trolling to the sides of the brush pile in an attempt to draw the more aggressive fish out to chase your fly. If this is accomplished it may trigger a competitive feeding binge but retrieving flies near the brush isn't the only tactic needed. The method can be performed by casting parallel to the edges of brush. Even from shore you can target three sides of the structure. Repetition will enable the caster to learn the perimeters of the brush pile. Another option is suspending the fly above the brush. Once again this method relies upon enticing a crappie to initiate the action by emerging from protective cover.

*Crappies have large eyes located on the tops of their heads. They are light-sensitive and look for food above their positions.*

If the crappies are located well down into the brush and refuse to come out the only remaining option is to go in after them. This is most effectively achieved by fishing vertically. Drop your weighted, weedless fly directly into the entanglements and allow it to fall all the way to the bottom. When bottom contact occurs remove the slack and lift the fly a few inches. Leave it there a few seconds before raising it again. When a branch is encountered, drop the rod tip to free the fly and allow it to fall, then lift the fly so that it flips over the branch. Strikes often come as the fly is freed from the limb. If the fly emerges from the brush pile without a hit move to another part of the same structure and repeat the process. This is a very methodical process which must be performed with finesse. Bumping into a branch with the fly is what you want to happen. Dropping the rod tip and bouncing the fly free is irresistible to crappies. It's the darting action created by the fly's escape that draws the fish's interest, but it must be performed very gently. Persistence with this method will pay dividends especially as the angler develops a "feel" for it. The sensitivity of the fly-rod tip delivers another real advantage for this type of fishing.

While it's entirely possible to catch crappies with the sun high overhead, conventional wisdom is that the best times to fish are connected to periods of diminished light. If you choose to fish in full sun, flies that incorporate a bit of flash and those of a fluorescent color are likely to produce best. This is because they reflect more light and can therefore be seen by the crappies at greater distances. Experience taught us, however, that this factor diminishes with depth. Below 10 to 12 feet, depending upon the intensity of sunlight penetration, fish are less responsive to these fly characteristics. Although we don't really know how crappies see a fly under those circumstances we have been told by divers that below those depths fly color tends to blend into a drab monochrome. If the fish's vision is similar to ours, at least in that respect, it could explain their reaction in depths exceeding about 12 feet.

We've experienced about equal success with both light and dark flies in deeper waters.

During the summer, crappies very often establish a pattern of feeding that begins as the sun gets low to the horizon and continues into the nighttime hours. Other crappie populations will begin feeding before sunup and continue into mid-morning. Anglers need to determine the most active feeding times on their waters to maximize fishing success. Most of us, however, are confined to going fishing when we have the time to do so. Unless you are able to hand pick those times you have to be versatile and flexible. We must be ready to fish shallow if the opportunity arises, to fish mid-depth suspended crappies or extremely deep if that's the only game in town. With that kind of versatility in mind it's a good idea to have outfits rigged and ready that are capable of addressing each of those areas of the water column. With gear ready to adapt to any crappie location we can be open to accepting those changes. The angler who goes to the lake with a preconceived notion of where the crappies are located and is so hard-headed as to stick with a single presentation is bound to experience slow fishing. Regardless of which part of the day you're fishing take a moment to assess the situation. What are weather conditions like? What is the extent of the sunlight penetration? What is the clarity of the water? If you've fished recently, what areas were successful and which were not? What kind of fishing pressure has this population of crappies been getting? Armed with the answers to these questions you can make an educated guess as to crappie location. Just don't become enamored with any particular location or a single presentation method.

## The Thermocline

In deep lakes during summer the water is separated into distinct horizontal temperature layers. This stratification produces three layers of water that remain intact throughout the summer and into early autumn. These three layers are known as the epilimnion, thermocline, and hypolimnion.

The epilimnion is a layer of warmwater which is oxygenated by wind action and is continually affected by air temperatures. The thickness of this layer of water depends upon a number of factors including air temperature, wind, and the size of the body of water.

The second layer is one of rapidly dropping water temperatures. Specifically the water temperature drops about one half degree Fahrenheit per foot.

*Brush piles are both a blessing and a curse to the crappie angler.*
*They can be tough to fish but that's where big ones hang out.*

Depth of the thermocline varies greatly. In large lakes with hundreds of feet of depth it might be 30 feet and become increasingly deeper as the summer progresses, while a small lake or pond sheltered from the wind might develop a thermocline at 10 to 15 feet that persists for the entire summer or may not stratify at all.

The hypolimnion is a cold-water layer which usually has very low oxygen content not capable of sustaining gamefish. The thermocline then becomes a summertime barrier that keeps fish above that depth. As such, it is a further aid to determining the depths of summer crappies.

## Using the Wind

Throughout the summer period wind gives a good indication of crappie location. Tiny plankton forms the bulk of the minnow population's diet. These micro-organisms are free floating and therefore are subject to the wind currents that develop. Crappie likely don't drift with this movement of their major food source, but instead the crappie population located on the windward side of the lake, pond or river simply become very active when the minnows or fry arrive in their area. If you're bank fishing, cast into the wind from the windward bank where the crappies' food will drift toward shore. Cast beyond the area where you suspect the crappies are feeding and retrieve the fly at a speed that replicates the current created by the wind.

*Huge schools of minnows or shad are a sure sign that crappies are nearby.*

Trolling into the wind slows the boat's movement, including your fly's presentation, and can be very effective. At the end of your trolling run cut the electric motor and drift back along the same path using the wind to propel the boat. Most often the trolling motor will need to be engaged periodically to keep the boat drift on the right path. This controlled drift can be especially productive because the boat is not only moving at the wind's speed but also because the wave action causes the fly to lurch erratically. If the breeze is not strong back-trolling may be a viable option because it enables the angler to more closely adhere to the weedline or other structure. This is only useful on a boat that is steered from the stern. With the transducer of the locator aimed from the area of the trolling motor it's possible to back troll in response to every subtle deviation in the structure's shape. This is particularly advantageous when crappies are relating very tightly to brush or weed lines and also when they locate very near bottom.

## Feeding the Insect Feeders

When crappies focus their attention on the abundant summer insect population they feed on emergers either as they begin their ascent from the bottom or as they arrive at the surface. If the latter is the case a short leader with one or more dropper rigs is an excellent way to catch fish. Fly-fishers can use a strike indicator to drift the fly or flies over the area, lifting the rod tip occasionally to replicate the insect's rise toward the surface. This lifting action performs a presentation known mostly to trout fishers as the "Leisenring lift." The flies should not be lifted with great speed, but instead with a slow and steady lift of the rod tip until the fly is nearly at the surface to allow the most realistic ascent. The lift must always be followed by a rather lengthy pause to allow the fly to resettle. When the fly or flies have reached their deepest point impart a series of twitches before reenacting the leisenring fift. Generally crappies are not selective as to the size or species of the insect imitation, but they are sometimes choosy about color. This may however, relate to the visibility of flies under the prevailing light conditions. As a result it's a good idea to start with a dropper rig using two or three different colors and even different fly patterns. If the fish show a decided preference for one fly or even for one depth switch your rig to accommodate their current appetites. Especially on calm summer evenings fishing the insect hatch can furnish outstanding action.

## Sunshine

*While not common, double hookups are possible on tandem rigs in the spring.*

Bright sunshine is the enemy of crappies, and consequently of fishermen, too. Usually the fish retreat to deep structure or suspend in the depths to avoid it. The irises of their eyes don't adjust to light changes like the human population's, so they remain quite deep until lower light conditions arrive in the form of cloud cover or lower angles of the sun. Sometimes this deep-water retreat forces inactivity on the fish. Some may need as much as 30 minutes to adjust to changing light conditions. For this reason the most difficult condition in which to locate fish is not the bright sunny day, but the days when the sun plays hide-and-seek among the clouds.

This may be as confusing to the fish as it is to fishermen. It may well be that after several false starts, the crappies simply become confused and wait until light conditions stabilize before resuming their feeding activity.

In one lake we fish regularly there is a very elongated point that juts for a hundred yards into the lake running north to south. The sides drop away sharply in both directions, which create a very unusual fishing situation. During the morning hours the west side of the point is shaded from the rising sun which affords the point good fishing even on bright summer days. Beginning in midafternoon the eastern side is shaded. The only hours of the day in this situation that expose both sides of the point to sunlight penetration is from about 10 am to 2 pm. Examine your waters for situations such as this one. You may have a submerged island or perhaps a mid-lake rock pile or even bridge pilings that afford protection from direct sunlight, and consequently an excellent locational tool on those bright days in the summer sun.

## Floating Markers

Floating markers are important in helping the angler return to suspended crappies. They can also be used to mark the spot where a crappie was caught. They can stake out submerged brush sites, manmade fish attractors, as well as humps, submerged islands, creek channels, deadfalls, and virtually any other crappie-attracting structure. Most operate very simply. They are equipped

with 50 feet or so of nylon cord which is wrapped around the marker itself for storage. When they are tossed overboard a heavy lead weight pulls the cord from the marker until it eventually comes to rest on the bottom. Floating markers come in several different sizes, colors, and shapes. As long as they are simple to rig and visible to the angler they will serve a valuable purpose.

*Brightly-colored floating markers are invaluable in marking structure.*

## Bayou Crappies

Many southern bayous may only average five feet in depth, but they are weed- and brush-filled and full of crappies. The water ranges from clear to the color of coffee grounds depending upon location and recent weather. The good news is that crappies are easy to locate. They are in the brush and weeds, pure and simple. The bad news is that the brush has a healthy appetite for flies. It can make for a miserable day. Casting is nearly impossible. The solution is vertical fishing or dipping. Use a fly with plenty of independent action and a weed guard. Lower your offering vertically through the branches until the fly is near the bottom before lifting the rod tip several inches. Impart a bit of action by flicking your wrist. If that fails to bring a strike, lower the rod tip, remove slack line, then lift the fly several more inches and repeat the action. If you feel a "hit" it may well be a branch. When this occurs drop the rod tip to free the fly and lift to bounce the fly over the limb. This may also be the action that triggers a strike.

Another viable option is casting weedless flies parallel to the deepest branches of the brush and, using a slow lift, drop, strip retrieve to entice crappies from the thickest entanglements.

## Pond Crappies

The weedline can be the key to locating crappies in ponds. If the weeds extend toward the deeper water far enough to make casting and working a fly difficult, a float tube can be the answer. Trolling, drifting, and controlled-drifting are just as viable in float tubes as in boats. It may also be possible to wade to the edge of the weeds and cast parallel to the weed line. Wading must be undertaken with great care in ponds where silted bottoms can pose the very real danger of trapping fishermen in deep mud.

## River Crappies

Stream-dwelling crappies locate in areas of diminished flow or those that are shielded by a current break. Look for deadfalls, weed beds, rock piles, and downstream points of islands or bridge pilings. If the waters aren't deep and the bottom is firm, wading may enable the angler to approach closely to the structure and allow delivery of short, accurate casts. If wading isn't possible a canoe, kayak or float tube may accomplish the same end. Small jig-type flies and Woolly Buggers, sizes 8 and 10, in black or yellow have given us the most action in summer streams.

# Night Fishing

In summer when daytime high temperatures are uncomfortably warm for fishermen and the waters are sun-drenched day after day, give night fishing a try. It allows anglers to avoid crowds and conflicts with water skiers and jet boats, as well as beat the heat. Especially in clear lakes, crappies tend to feed from dusk to dawn and move shallower to do so. Sometimes these shallow feeders, especially on calm nights, may feed just under the surface. In that situation short casts with soft splashdowns and erratically retrieved streamers may be all that's needed to stay in the action.

In dark-water environments the situation may be reversed. Crappies may feed all day long, but because their vision is limited they are forced to feed by utilizing senses other than their eyesight. Even in these darkened waters crappies will likely be more aggressive at night.

It's extremely important that night fishermen simplify their equipment and their tactics. Anglers must be highly organized. Boat fishermen that grope about in the dark, banging equipment against the gunwales and bottom of the boat are defeated before they start, while shorebound anglers can easily misplace needed equipment or stumble and break a favorite rod or other valuable piece of equipment. At night, keep your gear in a prearranged location and don't deviate from trip to trip. Move about slowly and deliberately. Confining yourself to one rod may be best but certainly it's important to have any outfits you intend to use completely rigged. A small head lamp can be invaluable when changing flies and tying knots, but care must be taken not to shine the light directly into the water. A number of years ago we experimented by using a portable black light, fluorescent fly line, and fluorescent leader material. The fluorescent leader material was purchased from the conventional-tackle aisle of a local sporting goods store. There's no question that the setup makes changing flies and tying knots easier in the darkness.

Easily the most important piece of nighttime equipment is a lantern or "crappie light", which attracts insects, micro-organisms, minnows, and other small fish to the surface. When this occurs the crappie population is certain to follow. There are two options in selecting a light for this purpose: 1. A gas-powered camping lantern rigged with reflector to direct the light toward the water (the kind we rented at an exorbitant price on Dale Hollow Lake. See Chapter 2); 2. A floating battery-operated crappie light. We set the battery for the light into a six-pack-sized cooler with a convenient handle, then we simply attach the electrodes to the battery post and set the floating light on the water's surface. Be sure to check if your state allows the use of these portable lights before using one. Don't overlook similar fish-attracting lights such as those on boat docks, marinas, boat houses, and bridges. They attract insects, minnows and crappies as well.

## Late Summer

As water temperatures begin to drop and sunlight hours begin to shorten crappies instinctively know that a major change is coming. Days may remain hot but night temperatures become cool. The entire ecosystem begins to slow down. No longer are insect and minnow populations continuing to reproduce. Water levels, particularly in rivers and streams, are often lower which forces the crappies to occupy deeper sections of the stream.

In late summer, crappies suspend less and congregate tightly to brush piles and weed lines. Anglers must use this tendency to form concentrated schools to our favor. Once located, many can usually be caught. Two presentation methods have been most successful for us in this situation. First, cast weedless jig-type flies directly into the brush pile, weeds, and fish attractors. Second, suspend a fly above the brush by using a slip bobber and imparting subtle action either by alternately lifting and lowering your rod tip or by using a gentle flick of the wrist.

As crappies relate even tighter to their entangled homes it may be necessary to employ a heavier leader tippet. The tippet can be in almost constant contact with wood branches or tough weed stems which can abrade the tippet and eventually force it to fail. Tippet strength of 5X may be fine for clear, open water but brush and weedbed fishing requires something heavier, say 3X. We prefer to fish with the lightest tippet we can comfortably use, but this is not the time to risk the break-off of a big fish. Check your tippet often by running it between your thumb and forefinger. If it feels rough or nicked, cut the affected part off and tie on a fresh tippet.

With the great abundance of the summer season coming to an end the crappie population cannot be quite so choosy about their menu. Many of the young-of-the-year fish species have by now outgrown their usefulness to crappies as a prey species. Crappies will feed more opportunistically now which results in fewer stubborn refusals. While the abundance of summer has waned the quality of the fishing has not.

### Jonesy and Ol' Red

For a small town in which many residents could be described as "characters" Jonesy was in a class by himself. He chain-smoked and drank too much, but his fishing prowess was legendary. He never held a job, lived in a tiny cabin in a wooded area near town, and drove a truck that was reminiscent of a rolling junk pile. Jonesy had a kind smile but spoke only when addressed. He was always in the company of a lop-eared reddish brown dog whose breed was questionable at best. Jonesy called him a "squirrel dog" and clearly there was enough hound in his background that he could and would hunt, but seemed ambivalent as to the quarry. The old mongrel always rode in the passenger seat of Jonesy's jalopy but frequently leaped through the open truck window if he spotted a cat worthy of a good chase. It was an event that always amused Jonesy. He would slow to watch the chase and readmit "Ol' Red" to the truck cab before proceeding to his destination at the breakneck speed of 20 mph.

One evening Terry drove along the dusty road that led to Jonesy's cabin only to find him and Ol' Red emerging from the timber. The old man was carrying a .22 rifle and two fat red squirrels.

He held them aloft, and smiled, "Whip up some squirrel gravy in a bit."

As Jonesy set about the task of cleaning the brace of squirrels, Terry sat on a stump and commented on the hunting prowess of the dog as a conversation starter.

"Yup," nodded Jonesy, "and he likes to fish, too."

Astonished by the statement, Terry asked if he meant that Ol' Red liked to go out in the boat with him.

"Nope," retorted Jonesy, "he shur'nuff points out da crappie."

Early the following morning Jonesy, Ol' Red, and Terry boarded a heavily dented jon boat in the drainage ditch behind the cabin. Creaking oar locks accompanied their lurches through darkened waters as a misty fog blanketed willows which lined the shore. It easily might have passed for a scene from Sir Arthur Conan Doyle's classic *The Hound of the Baskervilles*. One could easily imagine Sherlock Holmes sneaking through the mist searching for clues.

Just as the first rays of light sparkled above the eastern horizon the ditch opened into an expansive slough with clusters of stumps and log jams scattered from one end to the other. A startled Great Blue Heron took flight squawking its disapproval as it disappeared over the tree line. Ol' Red joined Jonesy on the skiff's front seat as the oars were abandoned in favor of a sculling paddle. Adept figure-eight paddle strokes propelled the boat silently until a series of emerging stumps were approached. Jonesy slowed the boat as Ol' Red leaned over the gunwale and stared intently at the rotten stump.

He paused for a few seconds and shook his head negatively before proceeding to the next stump. Here, Ol' Red repeated his actions at the first stump but this time emitted a series of excited whimpers.

"Ah-ha," smiled Jonesy as he reached for his fiberglass fly rod.

Attached to the business end was a 1/16-ounce jig which was immediately lowered along the stump's near side. After a couple of flicks of his wrists he lifted the lure from the water only to re-enter along the stump's backside. Suddenly the rod bent toward the water's surface as Jonesy lifted his

10-inch silver prize aboard. He hugged and patted Ol' Red. Both seemed exceedingly pleased with their collaborative efforts and proceeded to perform their magic until mid-morning when Jonesy again resumed his position on the oars at mid-ship with Ol' Red curled at his feet.

Upon arriving at home Terry confided that he didn't know exactly what he'd just witnessed. He certainly had no intention of telling his friends for fear his sanity would be called into question. But where does the truth lie? Could Ol' Red really point crappies? Or did Jonesy create a perfect hoax? He only dropped his lure into the water when Ol' Red whimpered but when he did, he always had a strike. Sometimes he appeared to miss the fish but he had caught plenty as well. So did Terry just witness a remarkable event or was he hornswoggled by Jonesy? You'll have to decide that one for yourself because thirty-five years later Terry still doesn't know.

## Chapter 5

# Cool- and Coldwater Crappies

A utumn is a wonderful time to be outdoors. The hillsides are splashed with gorgeous color, the sky is a brighter blue, and the air is crisp. Waterfowl have begun their annual southward migration, water skiers have stored their boats, and that old flannel shirt feels pretty good again. But in the lakes that have stratified into layers of differing water temperatures during summer, early fall is a time of great turmoil for the crappies as the lake turns over. This process begins as the warmer and lighter surface water rapidly cools. This cooling process is accelerated by cold rains and wind. As the surface water gets colder and therefore heavier, it sinks forcing the bottom layer of water to the surface. Further, wind action mixes the water together until the temperature of the water top to bottom is the same. This is called "the turnover," and it usually lasts from several days to a week or more. Often the lake actually has an unpleasant odor as bottom debris and decomposing vegetation are brought to the surface.

This is a very stressful time for the entire fish population, but it's especially so for crappies. This is because they have been suspended over deep water when the process takes place. Bass and bluegills, on the other hand, are often located in the weedlines near wood structure on the shallow flats. Their world grows substantially cooler to be sure, but they are less affected by the upheaval taking place in deeper areas of the lake than the crappies. Needless to say, crappie fishing during the turnover period is very difficult. Some of the crappie population may have migrated into the shallows, and therefore slowly fished flies in the weeds or brush may produce some satisfactory results if one is unfortunate enough to be fishing this situation. Fortunately there are some better choices available. Remember, not all bodies of water develop a thermocline. Rivers do not, and smaller lakes that are protected from the wind do not stratify and therefore don't turn over. So while the crappie population adjusts to the tumultuous events on the big lakes, successful crappie enthusiasts will pursue them in rivers and smaller waters.

For many this is the best time of the year to fish rivers. They can be at their lowest levels of the year which can confine crappies to the deepest holes with little current. It can also enable the angler to access structure that is more difficult at earlier times of the year. Streams that feed into large lakes and reservoirs can provide outstanding fishing.

One of our favorite streams for fall crappies feeds a large reservoir that serves as a water supply source for the area's largest city. Without unseasonably heavy rains through the summer months the lake and lower portion of the streams that feed it are several feet lower than normal. This enables fly-fishermen the opportunity to wade sections of stream that are far too deep to do so earlier in the year. Areas that remain too deep to wade can be accessed by kayaks or canoes. Current is very sluggish in these river sections where the banks are lined with deadfalls, brush, and stumps. As the water begins to cool, crappies enter the mouth of the river and migrate upstream to feed on aquatic insects and minnows. A simple marabou jig-type minnow imitator can catch many and if there is just a bit of current flowing up against some dead wood, a naturally drifted nymph pattern can produce excellent action.

To probe the deepest holes, try trolling or controlled-drifting using a fly with a tiny 00 spinner blade. Usually moving very slowly through the area and lifting, then lowering the rod tip will produce fish, but if the fish are hugging the bottom a section of sink-tip line will keep the fly down. A hit can sometimes feel like a hang-up but lifting the rod tip will reveal whether it's a fish or a snag. If it's a snag try back-trolling to free the fly; if it comes free allow it to continue to tumble along the bottom. Strikes often occur after the fly has been freed from a hang-up. If the stream is particularly snag-filled and the hang-ups too frequent, use a weed guard. Of course, with any weedguard system it's possible to wedge the fly between two forks of a branch or between a pair of rocks but these should be minimal with whatever weedguard the angler chooses. Obviously it's preferable not to use a weedguard. By leaving the hook exposed more positive hookups will be achieved, but if conditions won't allow it a weedguard is the answer. There are many times that retrieving the fly along the outside of the entanglements in the area free of hang-ups simply will not interest the fish. In that instance the only option is to go into the heaviest cover.

One tactic utilized by many veteran crappie fishermen requires the use of a soft, fine-wire hook tied as a jig and lowered vertically. When structure is felt the angler can lift the fly a few inches above the entanglement and either let it sit perfectly still or cause it to quiver in order to attract crappies. If the hook is snagged the soft-wire hook enables the fisherman to pull steadily upward so that the hook bends and comes free. Of course this requires a sturdy tippet and the hook must be reshaped before offering it to the crappies again.

Rivers, especially those that are connected to major lakes and impoundments, can that attract and hold some of the largest crappies of the year. Even though the water is much cooler and the air temperatures take a plunge, crappies are more aggressive under low light conditions. This can be proven by fishing structure in full sunlight, then as late-afternoon shadows reach across the stream cast to the same areas. If you keep score it won't even be close, unless the depths are significant.

Another alternative is to seek out smaller waters. Ponds may not stratify into layers separated by temperature and therefore not experience the turbulence of the turnover. As in river fishing, the crappie population in these smaller waters are far easier to locate and catch, but their waters also cool at much faster rates and will advance through the season faster. In both natural and impounded waters that fit this profile crappies' locations will be very similar. Look at the dying weedline near shore. As those weeds begin to die back there will be a band of healthy weeds near the edge of the first breakline. If this situation exists the crappie population will school very tightly within those weeds. Drop small flies into the pockets and along the edges of the healthy weeds. This can be accomplished either by vertically fishing each pocket with a slip bobber setup or on a tight line. Another option is back-trolling very slowly along the outside edges of the healthy weeds.

Chartreuse is a great fish-catching color for nearly all species, including crappie. In our experience this is especially true in cooler waters. Chartreuse alone and in combination with white seems to offer an edge for the angler. Fly size is also an important consideration at this time. Smaller flies, sizes 6 through 10, produce the best results. After finding good action in rivers and smaller lakes the angler may be forced to consider continuing to fish these areas even after turnover is complete on large waters. That's understandable, as both situations will continue to hold good fishing until the river fish return to the lake and the healthy weedline deteriorates in small lakes.

## Late Fall

Eventually even the deepest weeds die back enough to discourage both the minnow population and, of course, the crappies and both vacate the premises. The big question is, "Where do they go?" The answer depends on what is available to them. If there is deep-water structure available such as rock piles, creek channels, standing timber or submerged islands, they will almost certainly use them. If those elements are not available crappies are likely to suspend at levels that provide comfortable temperatures with prey species nearby.

While locating these late-fall suspended crappies can be challenging remember that the colder water has slowed their metabolism, which means they won't have travelled very far. Begin the search in confined open water near shallow areas they used earlier in late summer. In natural lakes those deeper areas may be within a few yards of the dying weedline they just abandoned or possibly the nearest confined open water. In reservoirs that support weedlines the locations may be the same, but in those that are devoid of weeds search the nearest deep water adjacent to the brush piles then gravitate to the nearest confined open water. Once located these late-fall crappies are very willing to feed but remember that their metabolism has slowed. They certainly are not willing to chase down a meal under those conditions. Once again fishing becomes a vertical operation. By very slowly back-trolling over the school a wider area can be covered without sacrificing the nearly stationary presentation these fish prefer. If the lake you fish has a lot of boat docks the docks can provide cover, shade, and structure to make a hotspot in late autumn. Keep in mind that not all docks are created equal. The best will be located near relatively deep water and contain brush or weeds as further inducement to hold crappies. Cast at various angles to support posts, under the floor of the dock if it's possible, and into the boat well. If the boat dock has a fish-cleaning station that has been used recently cast under it. Like other gamefish, crappie are not averse to making a meal of their departed brethren.

Many boat-dock owners drop their pine or cedar Christmas trees tethered to cement blocks off the dock's corners or ends to attract crappies. If there is a bench or some chairs on the dock it's likely they are positioned to fish the submerged trees. Check all around the dock to see if a tree pile exists. If so, fish it carefully.

On many northern natural lakes and an equally high number of mid-South impoundments there are mid-lake rock piles that can attract late-autumn crappies. These areas can furnish some of the best and some of the easiest fishing of the entire fall. Many times these deep rock piles attract large crappies, yet despite all these advantages many anglers don't fish them because they either don't know the submerged rock piles exist or they don't expect to find crappies there. In fact, if the rocks rise near enough to the surface to capture some sunlight there will be algae growing on the rocks which will attract the micro-organisms that minnows feed upon, which in turn attracts

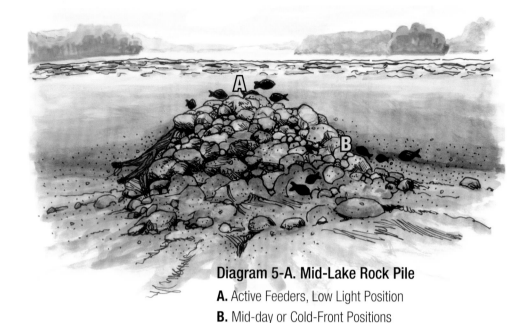

**Diagram 5-A. Mid-Lake Rock Pile**
**A.** Active Feeders, Low Light Position
**B.** Mid-day or Cold-Front Positions

crappies. That is an ideal crappie hot spot that will not only fish well in late fall but throughout the entire year. (See Diagram 5-A).

Many ponds have riprap facing along their dams. Especially if there are deadfalls or weeds in the corners of the dam, the area may attract crappies for much of the year. Jig-type flies are often best in these locations because they can be hopped up and down the face of the dam. The dam area can be fished from several different angles either from the bank or from the water with a small craft. If the pond is silted, check out the silt pile around the mechanical spillway. Over time weeds will take root there and small branches may have been deposited around it. Spillways also offer many angles for presentation. Cast to the deepest parts first and work progressively shallower to reduce the possibility of scaring the crappies. (See Diagram 5-B).

Finding a rock pile is tantamount to locating your own private crappie hole, which obviously makes time spent in the search well worth the effort. The first method for finding such a spot on big lakes is a studying a topographic map of the lake. Mark the areas where submerged rock piles might be located. Next take your marker buoys and the marked lake map and do some reconnaissance on the area with a locator. If you can find a potential hotspot, mark the top or shallowest part of the rock pile to determine if it falls within the depth of sunlight penetration. If so, mark the size and shape of the rock pile by triangulating the

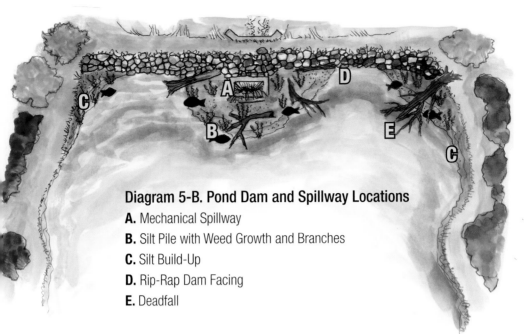

**Diagram 5-B. Pond Dam and Spillway Locations**
**A.** Mechanical Spillway
**B.** Silt Pile with Weed Growth and Branches
**C.** Silt Build-Up
**D.** Rip-Rap Dam Facing
**E.** Deadfall

location with permanent landmarks so that you can return to the area. If you intend to fish the place at night it's worth returning after dark to triangulate again using distant lights to facilitate your return there.

Often these rock-pile fish are located very close to the rocks. During times of heavy sunlight penetration the fish usually locate along the slope of the pile waiting for low light to move up on top to feed. Again because of their reduced metabolism the fly must be presented very slowly. Back-trolling with an electric motor is a good option or if the breeze is gentle enough a controlled drift can be employed. On calm days directly casting to the rock pile can be effective, but use the electric motor to keep the boat in position as anchoring to the rock pile is almost certain to spook the entire school.

In low-light conditions, start by casting or drifting to the top of the rock pile. If there is no action move progressively deeper until fish contact is made. Once again small-sized flies produce best. Many times we've used flies we normally fish for bluegills on sizes-10 to -12 hooks.

If crappies cannot be located in close proximity to the rock pile they are very likely suspended horizontally to the rocks. Locating them can be frustrating and time-consuming but the only option is to expand the search in ever-widening circles around the rock hump. It's very helpful to mark the length and width of the rocks with marker buoys. Otherwise it's very easy in open water to wander off track. Be sure to save a buoy or two so that when the school is located they can also be marked.

## Standing Timber

Many reservoirs of all sizes, including ponds, are filled with timber left standing. These can be crappie hotspots, but like docks not all standing timber is created equal. A single tree devoid of all its branches will hold few crappies, but those with multiple extending limbs will furnish cover for an entire school. Don't be fooled by branchless tree tops above the water line. It's what's beneath the surface that provides cover. Depending upon weather conditions crappies may be located high in the tree branches or at any depth that suits their needs and comfort at the time. If the water temperature is comfortable near the surface and cloud cover blocks sunlight penetration, or especially if a prey species is located there, crappies will relate to the highest branches of the tree. At another time sunlight penetration might force them to position along the middle branches of the tree while post-cold front conditions might force them to retreat to the protection of the deepest branches.

Tree-top presentations are very much vertical fishing situations. Weedless jig-type flies with some heft lowered directly into the branches then fished still, quivered, and yo-yoed in combination to see which is most attractive to the fish is best. It's necessary to experiment at different depths using the countdown method until fish contact is made. The water temperature will determine the

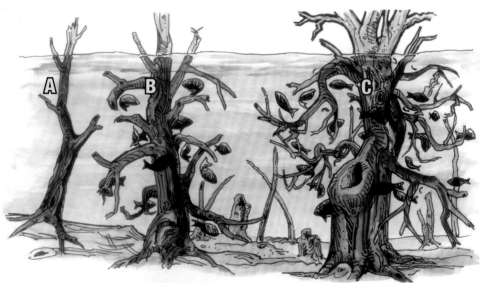

## Diagram 5-C. Typical Standing Timber in Reservoirs
**A.** Provides a Little Cover and Few Fish
**B.** Over-looked hot-spot because top is sparse but subsurface is good
**C.** Obvious Crappie Location

activity level of the crappies but usually by late fall fishing standing timber is a very precise and methodical procedure.

In most situations submerged standing trees must be fished from watercraft. We regularly fish a small pond with standing timber from float tubes in cold water. Layered clothing is important certainly, but the increased maneuverability is a definite advantage. (See Diagram 5-C). Don't be fooled into believing that all standing timber is the same. The key to each tree's suitability is multiple submerged branches. Sometimes the portion of the tree that is above the waterline is deceiving. It can appear sparse while the submerged portion is excellent crappie cover. These can be overlooked hotspots even in reservoirs that are heavily fished.

## Fly Color

Ask ten crappie aficionados about their most productive lure colors and it's a near certainty that you'll get ten different answers. Blending many of these colors with chartreuse seems to enhance the fly's attractiveness. Plain chartreuse flies are effective, as are chartreuse over white and chartreuse over yellow. Black over chartreuse comes close to being a year-around favorite, but there are times that a plain blue fly is unbeatable. Pink or fluorescent pink and flashy silver flies are popular in spring. It's always a good idea to continue to change fly colors if the catching is slow.

## Winter

As the late fall coldwater season progresses into winter some reservoirs from the mid-South northward become locked in ice. While crappies continue to feed, as the ice-fishing crowd can attest, this is not a situation for the fly-fisher so we'll focus on southern opportunities. Winter brings the coldest water temperatures of the year, and it's common for several pods of crappies to join together and form a massive school. This can be both a curse and a blessing for the angler. These coldwater crappies tend to be tightly schooled and therefore more difficult to find, but once located they are willing feeders and good numbers can be caught in the same area. Another factor worth considering when faced with the task of searching for them is that it's common for some truly large crappies to be caught in cold-water situations.

If an impoundment is deep, with many elements of structure, it is likely subject to having the water drawn down several feet in preparation for anticipated spring rains. In this case the minnow population and the crappies are pulled toward deeper water and will likely suspend horizontally in relation to deep structure. Their decreased metabolism and deep location enforces a vertical slow, even stationary, presentation. Best results usually come by simply lowering a weighted fly to just above the crappies' position. Hold the rod still for 20 seconds or more, then strum the line near the reel as if playing a guitar to cause the fly to quiver. However, if the fly is taken as it drops into position, or within just a few seconds of its arrival, this may indicate an active feeding period for these fish. If this is the case a slow back-trolling presentation might engage the school to feed competitively. Another possibility is drifting very slowly over the population if the breeze is gentle. Irrespective of the increased activity of this school the presentation must be very slow. In almost no case will stripping line or yo-yoing the fly be attractive to these cold-water fish.

If your southern crappie water is shallow, either in the form of a backwater lake, oxbow or the natural lakes in Florida, fish location can be simplified. The deepest water in many of these waters is 10 to 15 feet. It simply amounts to finding the lake's deepest water and identifying its perimeters. Again marker buoys can be invaluable to this process. It's always important to triangulate the area so that return trips can locate it easily.

The shallow-lake winter crappies suspend within two to three feet of the bottom so it's important to keep your fly in that area, but without dragging the bottom. Most often these areas have silted bottoms and creating a silt cloud tends to turn crappies off. Trolling minnow imitations can be successful but depth control can be problematic. If there is a chop on the water trolling into the wind may help keep the fly in the fish zone. A short section, 10 feet or less, of sinking line or a sink-tip with a short sinking tip can also be effective in putting and keeping the fly in the fish zone.

Water temperatures can indicate how fast the trolling speed needs to be, and certainly this is a function to some degree of latitude and, of course, local weather. If the water's temperature is in the low-40's trolling speeds must be much slower than they would be in a lake which has a mid-January temperature in the mid- to upper-50's.

Shallow-lake winter crappies may also be a good situation to try trolling a cast of two or even three streamers. Tightly compacted populations are accustomed to seeing schools of minnows and they are more aggressive when attacking a minnow cluster. Although it doesn't happen often in cold water, a multiple hookup is possible. In a three-fly-cast we prefer to knot the first and

*Autumn is a great time to wade a slow-moving river for crappies.*

*Crappies school more tightly in cold water enabling*
*anglers to catch many once they're located.*

lightest unweighted fly to the leader conventionally then attach a length of tippet to the same hook eye, extending it perhaps 12 to 18 inches before tying on the second fly. The third fly should be the heaviest of the three but not so heavy as to be difficult to keep off the bottom.

In many areas of the South there are small lakes near rivers created by dredging low-lying land to build levees for flood prevention. These are called "borrow pits" or sometimes "bar ditches." When the river floods it empties water and fish into the bar ditch and often these become excellent crappie fisheries. These bar ditches have the same characteristics as the oxbows previously described, so the same locations and presentations apply.

Another similar situation occurs in manmade ditches through low-lying crop lands created for the purpose of either draining the fields or providing water for irrigation. Some of these ditches have a permanent water supply and enough depth to make a viable fishery like the bar ditches. Again the deepest areas will host the crappies in cold water. Often the deepest areas of these drainage canals are at the location where two of them intersect. Fishing these dark-water gems can be accomplished either with a small pram or by walking the banks. Some are on public right-of-ways but many are on private property. If the ditches run under a roadway it's possible to access them by boat in some states. Make sure to check your state's regulation before exploring these fisheries.

When surface temperatures plummet below 40 degrees most crappie schools seek deep water between 20 feet and perhaps as deep as 35 feet. But there are

*River fishing can provide great action. Look for areas of submerged wood.*

times when schools will occupy shallow structure in water from 4 to 10 feet. They may also suspend at that depth near the structure. When the locator cannot find schools that are especially deep it's a good idea to check out some of the prime shallow hotspots to see if the fish have been drawn to that area. If so, they will likely be actively feeding but are sluggish enough that only a very slow presentation has a chance of being successful.

On days when the crappies are clustered tightly to wood structure, use a weedguard on your fly to prevent constant hang-ups. Lower a weighted fly without a slip bobber or strike indicator directly into the brush and use the rod to lift the fly slowly toward the surface. This needs to be done very gently while being fully conscious of the "feel" of the fly. Crappies much prefer a dropping fly as opposed to one that is rising unless the fly is representative of an emerging insect. While this is one way to denote the difference between bumping into a branch and having a crappie bite, anglers that are sensitive to this feel will quickly learn the difference. This presentation must be accomplished with finesse.

It's also important to realize that often crappies may occupy only a small percentage of the brush. Many anglers make the mistake of fishing the structure when they need to be much more specific than that to be successful. Just fishing over the top of the brush may not interest a single fish. If the crappies are tightly schooled they might only occupy 10 percent of the structure. To put fish in the boat the angler must locate that 10 percent. This is very much an all or nothing procedure. If several fish are caught and they suddenly quit biting try resting the area by fishing another piece of structure or back off the structure and tie on a new fly. Usually after 10 to 20 minutes the fish's interest will be renewed and a new fly or even just a color change can trigger another round of relatively fast action.

## Chapter 6

# A Few Good Flies

*The simple Woolly Bugger is an excellent attractor pattern used for mid-depth and deep water fishing."*

Fly-fishermen understand that there are no silver bullets when it comes to flies. Relying on just one fly for any species is limiting and fly selection for crappies is no different. The most important statement anyone can make about any fly for any species is that all flies are situational. Crappies in particular may be located on the shallow flats, suspended near the flats, in the weeds, suspended near the weeds, in the brush, suspended near the brush, suspended in confined open water, on rock piles in mid-lake or located near bottom. No one fly is capable of addressing each of those situations with the best possible presentation. Fortunately there are thousands of fly patterns that are capable of catching crappies under some circumstances some of the time, and that is a large part of the problem. It's like going to an ice cream shop that has an infinite number of flavors. How do you choose the flavor that is going to satisfy your sweet tooth at that moment? There are seven fly characteristics that should be considered when selecting a fly for one of these situational presentations. Color can be an important criterion that relates more to the fish's ability to see it under the light penetration and water clarity combinations at that moment. Fly shape and size also plays a role in either tempting or discouraging the crappie's appetite. Action, often independent action, such as the slight movement of marabou for example, can be the trigger for a crappie's attack. The fly's weight, its descent rate, and even angle of its descent can be compelling triggers for our quarry as well.

To answer the question of which fly to use under which conditions we must analyze each fishing situation while taking into account the problems that may accompany each choice. It's obvious that choosing a cork popper to fish over crappies suspended at 15 feet will entice few strikes. But many choices aren't so cut and dried. For that reason we have created a series of flies that address each of the crappie fishing situations we've discussed. We'll discuss each and how we've used them, but understand that we're not trying to promote ourselves in so doing. There are hundreds of flies (more likely thousands) that are capable of performing the same tasks. Choose whatever flies you have confidence in, but by all means understand what qualities that fly contributes to the situation you're fishing.

If you are interested in tying some of our original flies, we're happy to share the recipe and tying instructions. We'll also give examples of other flies that perform the same function. Some of these flies represent specific foods from the crappies' menu, while others are impressionistic, tied to represent broad categories of edible organisms. Still others are classified as attractor patterns because, while effective, they represent no real critters. The versatile fly-fisher will want representatives of each major category and know when and how to fish them.

Virtually any piece of material lashed to a hook will catch a few fish some of the time. Our mission, however, is to capture more and do it consistently, so we'll confine this discussion to only those flies that we've found to be good producers.

### Flies for Casting to Surface Feeders

Many years ago our first fly-rod-caught crappie fell for a cork popper—a red one. It was an accidental catch because we expected to catch bluegills there as we had previously, but on that day the shallow weeds near shore held lots of crappies. Since we had just purchased the red popper at the local hardware store that sudden crappie explosion was attributed to the color of the fly. That, of course, had nothing to do with it, and eventually we learned that the crappies were guarding nests in very clear shallow water. It was a rather uncommon event. Most of the time a surface fly is a poor choice for crappies, but in this one instance with clear water and very shallow spawning crappie it was dynamite. As a result of this experience we always carry a few surface flies in the spring. Our first choice is our version of a Sponge Spider because it lands very softly on the water's surface, has great action with its rubber legs, and it's red micro chenille butt provides a contrasting target for the rising fish. Wilson's Sponge Spider should be cast to a likely shallow target and allowed to sit motionless until the splashdown rings disappear. Next, try shaking the rod tip gently from side to side. This causes the fly to activate the legs very slightly without moving forward substantially. We call this tactic "quivering." If the fly still hasn't attracted a bite, impart a 2-inch strip before letting it rest again. We tie our Sponge Spider in three different colors: yellow, chartreuse, and black. Notice a totally red-bodied Sponge Spider wasn't included. It takes a bit of experimentation to determine which color the crappies prefer, usually due to variances in water clarity and sunlight penetration.

## Wilson's Sponge Spider

(Colors: Yellow, chartreuse, black)
*Hook:* Mustad 94840, size 10
*Thread:* 140 denier or 6/0,
color to match body
*Butt:* Red micro chenille
*Body:* Midge Sparkle Braid
*Hackle:* Size 14 neck hackle
*Rib:* Small gold Ultra Wire
*Legs:* Grizzly barred rubber legs
*Carapace:* 3/16-inch closed-cell foam

## Tying Instructions

**Step 1:** Cut closed-cell foam to 1/4-inch width. Make "V" cut at one end so attachment to the hook will be smooth.

**Step 2:** Secure thread to hook bend.

**Step 3:** Attach closed-cell foam by wrapping along the "V" shape and allow it to lie beyond the hook bend.

**Step 4:** Attach the red micro chenille in front of the closed-cell foam. Make one wrap and secure with thread. Cut the excess chenille close to the hook shank.

**Step 5:** Attach the Ultra Wire, neck hackle, and sparkle braid.

**Step 6:** Wrap the thread to the hook eye and half hitch.

**Step 7:** Advance the Midge Sparkle Braid to near the hook head, but leave room to attach the legs. Half hitch.

**Step 8:** Palmer the hackle to the same location behind the head and half hitch.

**Step 9:** Spiral the Ultra Wire through the hackle and secure at head.

**Step 10:** Lay two lengths of grizzly barred round rubber legs across the top of the hook shank in the space left in an "X" extending at approximately 30 degrees from the hook shank and secure with thread.

**Step 11:** Pull the closed-cell foam over the body and secure with thread. Cut the closed-cell foam so that it creates a head that extends one-fourth the length of the hook shank beyond the hook eye.

**Step 12:** Wrap the thread under the extended head, double whip finish and cut the thread. Trim the legs so that each is approximately two hook shank lengths.

Any similarly sized popper achieves the same results. Use the popping sound sparingly, however, because these fish are very shallow in clear water and scare easily. Another viable choice is a size-8 or -10 Humpy. It will land with a softer splashdown than a popper and can be quivered effectively, but it's a bit less attractive with a strip-and-pause retrieve. These surface flies will likely be the least used of your crappie arsenal, but on the occasions when they can be fished effectively their use delivers a magical experience that satisfies the desire we all have to see fish take flies off the water's surface.

### Flies for Casting to the Shallow Flats

When spring crappies first invade the shallows they have done so because they followed a food source. Small minnows and shad are usually the target. When we initially realized that minnows were the preferred prey we began selecting early twentieth-century classic streamers like Black Ghost, Black Nose Dace, and others to cast and strip across the flats. Eventually we chose a more modern streamer created by Keith Fulsher in the 1960's. It's one in a series of bucktail streamers tied in the reverse style created by the legendary Carrie Stevens. Fulsher's streamers are called the Thunder Creek series. These flies are a clear departure from the earlier, more ornate, and often overdressed flies to smaller and more sparsely dressed creations. The older classics, as well as the Thunder Creek Bucktails, remain just as effective but we've chosen to take simplicity one step further. Our small streamer, Mini Minnie, is an impressionistic streamer that utilizes marabou for action and Quick Descent Dubbing for a little weight and some flash.

## Mini Minnie

(Colors: Silver/white, copper/olive)
*Hook:* Tiemco 200R, sizes 10 or 12
*Thread:* 70 denier or 8/0, color
to match the tail and wings
*Tail:* Marabou
*Body:* Quick Descent Dubbing
*Rib:* Small Ultra Wire
*Wing:* Marabou
*Gills:* Red thread, 140 denier or 6/0
*Head:* Bead head, 1/8-inch diameter

## Tying Instructions

**Step 1:** Thread bead head onto hook and push to hook eye.

**Step 2:** Secure thread at hook bend.

**Step 3:** Secure a small bunch of marabou half the length of the hook shank at tail. Cut off excess.

**Step 4:** Secure small Ultra Wire.

**Step 5:** Using the thread-core direct dubbing method, dub the body with Quick Descent Dubbing.

**Step 6:** Spiral the small ultra-wire rib to behind the head and trim the excess.

**Step 7:** Secure a small bunch of marabou behind the head that extends to the end of the tail, trim the excess. Half-hitch the thread behind the bead head and cut.

**Step 8:** Secure the red thread behind the bead head; make several wraps to form the gills. Whip finish and cut thread.

These streamers should be stripped slowly and erratically across the flats to entice crappies that are feeding on minnows. Another productive retrieve is one we call the "lift, drop, strip." It's performed simply by raising the rod tip a few inches then dropping it to its original position and stripping only to remove the slack line. This creates an undulating action that demands the attention of the crappies because it replicates a wounded minnow struggling to survive. That's irresistible even for crappies with slowed metabolisms. The silver/white represents a small minnow and the copper/olive a small sunfish.

## Flies for Casting to Weeds, Brush
## Piles, Stumps, and Deadfalls

If the angler has determined that crappies are using the edge of a weedbed or hovering above brush it's possible to present flies near, but not in, the structure. In this instance it's preferable to use flies without weedguards. If hang-ups become more than a minor annoyance or if the fish are located in the weeds or wood branches, a weedguard will then be necessary. This situation calls for a fly that descends through the water column slowly because crappies in these positions generally prefer a meal that is dropped into their lairs as opposed to lifted away from them.

Lightly-weighted Woolly Buggers and bead-head flies that use marabou or flexible synthetic hair perform well in this arena. Again, the lift, drop, strip retrieve causes the fly to drop toward the fish's position several times within each cast and covers different levels of the water column. One of our flies that has performed especially well for us both in and over structure is a fly we call Crappie Bully. It's a larger version of one of our bluegill flies, Bully's

Bluegill Spider. Its rubber legs slow the fly's descent and wiggle seductively as it approaches the crappies' field of vision. Its silver body, wide-gap hook, and exposed gills make it particularly attractive to these more aggressive fish. Again it's a very simple tie.

## Crappie Bully

(Colors: Silver)
*Hook:* Mustad 3366, sizes 6 and 8
*Thread:* 140 denier or 6/0, white
*Weight:* .020 lead wire
or the equivalent
*Body:* Holographic Chenille, silver
*Gills:* Red chenille
*Legs:* Medium round
rubber hackle, white

## Tying Instructions

**Step 1:** Attach the thread at the hook bend and run a line of thread to the fly head and back.

**Step 2:** Secure a line of .020 lead wire along the tier's side of the hook shank spiraling thread to the head and back.

**Step 3:** Complete 3 wraps of the lead wire on the back third of the hook shank.

**Step 4:** Make a fourth or transitional wrap to the head.

**Step 5:** Make the fifth wrap just behind a space left to tie in the legs. Cut the lead.

**Step 6:** Attach the Silver Holographic Chenille at the hook bend and advance the thread to the head position. Wrap the Silver Chenille forward to behind the head, secure with thread, and cut off the excess.

**Step 7:** Secure the red chenille and form a ball by completing two side-by-side wraps and then a third "soft" wrap over the center of the two previous wraps. Cut the excess.

**Step 8:** Cut two strips of white round rubber hackle approximately two inches in length.

**Step 9:** Secure these two rubber hackle strips just in front of the chenille ball with the lengths of rubber hackle lying in the same direction of the hook shank.

**Step 10:** Take two of the legs between thumb and forefinger on each hand and twist the legs so that two lie along the backside of the hook shank (far side to the tier) and two on the tier's side of the hook shank. Pin them in that position with one hand (the left for right-handed tiers) and build a base of thread which traps the legs between the head and the body.

**Step 11:** Release the legs. They may point in an unwanted direction either individually or collectively. Consider them to be infinitely adjustable as each leg can be pulled into a more favorable position then locked into place by running thread behind then in front of the leg. Whip finish the head and clip the thread.

The way in which the lead wire is wrapped allows the fly to sink at approximately a 45-degree angle, butt first, which activates the legs both as it falls through the water and as it is stripped.

Another of our original flies used to fish structure is one we call Wilson's Brim Reaper. It's performed especially well in and along deadfalls in streams, canals, bar ditches, ponds, and bayous.

## Wilson's Brim Reaper
(Colors: yellow, black)
*Hook:* Mustad 94840, size 10
*Thread:* 70 denier or 8/0 color to match the body
*Tail:* Medium round rubber hackle, furled
*Body:* Uni-Yarn
*Rib:* Small red wire
*Collar:* Senyo Shaggy Dub
*Eyes:* Extra small bead chain eyes (5/64 diameter), gold
*Head:* Super Bright Dubbing
*Front Thread:* 140 denier or 6/0, red

## Tying Instructions

**Step 1:** Attach thread at the hook bend and wrap to head position and back.
**Step 2:** Secure a length of small red wire.
**Step 3:** Furl a 2-inch piece of medium round rubber hackle by grasping

each end between the thumb and forefinger of each hand. Twist the ends in opposite directions so that the rubber hackle curls on itself, thus creating a single length of rubber hackle that is now double in thickness.

**Step 4:** Grasp the end of the furl to prevent it from unraveling and secure with thread creating an extended tail that is the same length as the hook shank.

**Step 5:** Advance the thread to just behind the head and secure a connected pair of extra-small gold bead eyes.

**Step 6:** With the thread behind the bead-chain eyes, secure a strand of Uni-Yarn. Advance the yarn to the hook bend and back, secure with thread and cut off excess.

**Step 7:** Spiral the red wire to behind the eyes.

**Step 8:** Tie in a small clump of Senyo Shaggy Dub behind the eyes and use your fingers to maneuver it halfway around the hook shank. Cut off excess.

**Step 9:** Turn the fly upside down. Tie in small clump of Senyo Shaggy Dub and use fingers to distribute half around the hook shank. Cut excess.

**Step 10:** Use the thread-core direct dubbing method to dub the head, clip to shape and whip finish. Cut thread. Attach red thread, make several wraps and whip finish.

We also tie a Woolly Bugger using peacock herl as the body reinforced with a gold wire rib. The tail is yellow/olive and the hackle is brown. A 1/8-diameter gold bead weights the fly.

## Trolling Flies

Flies used for trolling might be needed to target suspended fish and at other times needed to reach bottom. Regardless, the same flies can be used for both, with the difference in depth controlled by both the weight of sinking line and speed control. These are flies that have some weight, and in body shape and flash represent a shad or minnow. Since they are meant to be trolled, a bit of extra weight on these flies helps keep the line tight and anglers won't need to be concerned with casting heavier or bulkier flies.

One of the most common flies used for trolling is a Clouser Deep Minnow. Remember you can adjust the weight of the fly by choosing the desired weight of the barbell eyes. For most mid-depth trolling we prefer a small (1/40-ounce. on floating line or 1/60 -ounce on full-sink line) eye but a deeper troll at the same speed requires a medium (1/30-ounce on full-sink line) barbell eye. All white, chartreuse over white, and gray over white all do well depending on how picky the crappie might be.

For suspended fish we make a short cast, then feed out about 40 feet of full-sink line and adjust our speed until we make fish contact. When that occurs repeat the length of the line, weight of the fly, and speed of the troll to return to that depth. When the crappies are located near bottom in deep water, lower your fly straight down until bottom contact is made, then either back-troll to ensure a slow trolling speed or use the electric motor intermittently to continue a nearly vertical presentation.

While using the same trolling technique for depth control, we like to use a fly we call Squirrel Spin. It has a 00 spinner blade attached at the hook bend, a flashy body, squirrel tail wing, and cone head. Even when it's trolled the fly angler can execute the lift, drop portion of the lift, drop, strip retrieve. This causes the fly to dive head first which activates the tiny spinner blade. This is especially effective when deep trolling. The long-line retrieve activates the spinner as it is pulled through the water.

## Wilson's Squirrel Spin

(Colors: Silver, gold)
*Hook:* Mustad 3366, size 4
*Thread:* 140 denier or 6/0
*Tail:* Colorado spinner blade size 00 with barrel swivel and split ring, color to match fly color
*Underbody:* Wool yarn, gray for silver, yellow for gold
*Body:* Quick Descent Dubbing, color to match fly color
*Rib:* Medium Ultra Wire
*Gills:* Red medium chenille
*Wing:* Clump of squirrel tail, gray squirrel for silver, fox squirrel for gold
*Head:* Small cone head, color to match body, add Quick Descent Dubbing behind head to fill the gap

## Tying Instructions

**Step 1:** Slip small cone head over the hook point and slide to head.

**Step 2:** Attach 00 Colorado spinner blade to a barrel swivel and split ring

**Step 3:** Tie in at hook bend and make several wraps both above and below the ring so that when attached the spinner extends straight away from the hook shank.

**Step 4:** Tie in medium Ultra Wire and wool yarn. Advance the wool to just behind the cone head, and then advance the thread to the same point over the wool. Wrap the wool back to the hook bend followed by the thread. Trim excess yarn close to the hook shank.

**Step 5:** Spin Quick Descent Dubbing on the same location, secure with thread, and trim excess.

**Step 6:** Tie in medium chenille, make two side-by-side wraps, secure with thread, and trim excess.

**Step 7:** Tie in clump of squirrel tail which should not extend beyond the hook bend.

**Step 8:** Add Quick Descent Dubbing wraps behind the head to fill in the gap. Double whip finish and trim excess thread.

The silver Squirrel Spin is best in relatively clear water while the gold pattern excels in stained water.

## Flies Under Strike Indicators

When crappies suspend over submerged islands, rock piles or brush piles they sometimes curiously reject larger, and especially moving flies. They seem to be intrigued only by small, bite-sized morsels that sit right in front of them without much action. In general these fish are suspended in relatively shallow water, perhaps six or eight feet over a 12-foot bottom, for example. They may in fact be there to feed on nymphs that are found in the area, but whether that's their objective or not there are many times that they will bite small insect imitations but refuse to take larger flies. It may be that it's the smaller size and rather still presentation they favor rather than a dietary change; but whatever the reason, presenting an insect pattern under a strike indicator can sometimes spell the difference between spending an evening with a bent rod or going fishless.

One impressionistic pattern that imitates many small emerging insects is a trout fisher's favorite, the Soft Hackle. It's an incredibly simple pattern consisting only of a thread body and a few wraps of a soft-hackle feather such as partridge to serve as legs. While trout fishers may fish these sparse patterns in sizes 14 and smaller, they work perfectly well for crappies in sizes 10 and 12.

It takes a fairly substantial strike indicator to float even these sparse, unweighted flies. Relatively calm waters are also necessary to effectively present these aquatic insects.

Our North Fork Nymph, originally tied for trout after a rock-turning foray, has its tail and abdomen tied with cock pheasant tail feathers like Sawyer's Pheasant Tail Nymph. On our fly the thorax is tied using dubbing, both to give it a spiky appearance and so that it is viewed by the fish in the round and not seen as being on its side or upside down. It's lightly weighted but can be tied without weight when that's necessary. We tie it in size 12 in two colors.

## Wilson's North Fork Nymph

*Colors:* Fiery red brown, electric blue
*Hook:* Tiemco 200R, size 12
*Thread:* 140 denier or
6/0, brown or blue
*Tail:* 4 strands of cock pheasant
tail, brown or dyed blue
*Abdomen:* Continuation of pheasant
tail wrapped to half the hook shank
*Rib:* Small Ultra Wire, copper or blue
*Weight:* 6 wraps of .020 lead wire or less
*Thorax:* Poul Jorgensen SLF dubbing, Fiery Red Brown or Electric Blue

## Tying Instruction

**Step 1:** Attach thread at the hook bend and wrap thread to eye and back.

**Step 2:** Tie in four strands of pheasant tail at the hook bend so that the tail is half the length of the hook shank.

**Step 3:** Tie in small wire.

**Step 4:** Wrap the remaining pheasant tail around the thread two times and advance the thread and pheasant tail along the hook shank approximately halfway to the hook eye.

**Step 5:** Spiral the small wire to the same spot. Cut excess wire.

**Step 6:** Make 6 wraps of .020 lead wires (optional) in the thorax area.

**Step 7:** Using the SLF dubbing dub over the lead wrapping and whip finish the head.

**Step 8:** Trim the thorax.

One of the world's premier popper fly tiers is Alabama native Walt Holman, who once confided to us that his favorite presentation was "do nothing, then do just a little bit." That's exactly how these strike-indicator flies need to be presented. Allow the crappies to stare at the motionless nymph for long seconds then simply strum the line as if it were a guitar string. This causes the fly to quiver and many of these insect feeders are triggered to bite when it occurs.

### Flies for Slip-Bobbering and Tight-Line Jigging

Even though slip-bobber fishing and tight-line jigging involve two separate presentations the same flies can be used. These flies need to have enough weight to get deep and either action that is independent of angler manipulation, a flashy appearance or both. Large bead-head Woolly Buggers tied with guinea fowl hackle perform well, as do Clouser Minnows tied with a synthetic fiber such as craft fur or hanks of SLF. Slip bobbers must have a method of stopping the slide of the bobber at the right depth. A pinch-on strike indicator does this well and can be the adjusted to other depths when that's necessary. Since the entirety of the line must be monofilament for the slip bobber to slide up and down we each have a spare spool rigged with 30 feet of mono line. It's necessary to add a length of smaller diameter monofilament to serve as the final connection between the fly and the heavier line. It enhances the fly's action and is less visible to the fish.

Tight-line jigging involves dropping the fly into a deep crappie lair. The structure such as brush, deadfalls, stumps or a pile of rocks can be felt as the fly is manipulated. Weedless flies are a must because they are fished directly in the entanglement. When structure contact is made simply drop the rod tip a few inches then bump the fly past the structure before allowing it to free-fall again. Often the bumping of the fly into the structure triggers the bite. The spool of monofilament line can be used for deep tight-line jigging, as well as slip-bobbering.

Our creation that has served well in this deep presentation is one we call Bass Bully.

## Bass Bully

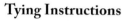

*Colors:* Chartreuse, black, olive, rust, gray
*Hook:* Mustad 3366, size 4
*Thread:* 210 denier or 3/0, color to match tail and body
*Body:* Large Ice Chenille, color to match tail
*Gills:* Medium red chenille
*Rubber Hackle:* Sili Legs, color to match tail and body
*Eyes:* Extra small barbell eyes or small eyes for heavier fly
*Head:* Stacked and trimmed sculpin wool, color to match body and tail

## Tying Instructions

**Step 1:** Secure the thread to the hook bend and advance to the head and back.

**Step 2:** Secure the rabbit strip. Make sure it is the same length as the hook shank. The rabbit strip should be inverted so the hair faces downward because the finished fly rides hook-point up.

**Step 3:** Secure the large Ice Chenille. Advance thread halfway along the hook shank. Wrap Ice Chenille to the same point, secure with thread and trim excess.

**Step 4:** Secure red chenille in front of the Ice Chenille and form a ball by wrapping two side-by-side wraps and a third wrap between the first two. The wraps should appear rounded like a ball. (The ball helps flare the legs of the fly and contributes a contrasting color target for a fish strike.)

**Step 5:** Select two full strips of Sili Legs. Cut in half to create two pair of legs tied with 4 legs on the bottom of the hook and 4 tied above. Tie them in place so they extend away from the hook shank at roughly a 90-degree angle.

**Step 6:** Using a figure 8 wrap attach the barbell eyes on top of the hook shank.

**Step 7:** Tie in 4 clumps of sculpin wool, one behind the eyes on top of the hook, one in front of the eyes on the bottom of the hook shank, one in front of the eyes on top, one behind the eyes on the bottom. Trim head to shape. Double whip finish the head and cut thread.

*Just one more cast.*

The chartreuse Bass Bully, as well as the black one, has performed well in these deep probes. Obviously designed as a bass fly, we pressed it into service tied on a size-4 hook and it produced when we were having difficulty inducing hits. It was immediately promoted to first-string status on deep crappies.

The list of flies needed for success on crappies is really quite small but each of the situations in which you find fish requires a fly that is well adapted to the circumstances. In smaller waters such as ponds, streams, canals, bayous, and bar ditches which are devoid of truly deep water, smaller flies are best. Sizes 8, 10, and 12 have the most appeal, even to larger specimens. Remember, every fly is situational.

*White with silver is a good color combination when crappies are focused on minnows or shad.*

## Chapter 7

# Putting It All Together

Putting together the pieces of the fishing puzzle properly means we can catch more crappies more often. Each trip to a lake, stream or pond is a test which presents a new set of variables that requires analysis and a response. Successful fishing trips confirm that we have analyzed the conditions correctly, chosen the right location, fly, and presentation. As complete crappie fly-fishers we want to be able to repeat good results in all seasons and in a wide variety of different conditions. There will be times of course when we'll be fooled. Even the best guides aren't successful every time out. But we should be able to learn from those failures and be able to keep them to a minimum.

### The Fishing Diary

While fishing regularly is a great teacher and usually leads to improved fishing success we've found that keeping a journal of our fishing trips enables us to see the results of our problem-solving. We've kept a fishing diary since 1968 and found it invaluable in analyzing our fishing methods, spotting how changes have either helped or harmed our results, and in seeing how patterns change with the weather and the seasons. As a result we've seen our methods evolve into the system that we use today. Diary keepers need to be sure to record the date, weather data, water conditions, and the quantity and quality of the catch. Include information about the fly patterns tried with hook size, color, and weight. Write a detailed description of your presentations and your positioning, and note the unsuccessful methods as well as the ones that produced fish. Reviewing these records at the end of the season or year will help in future planning. In analyzing the year, it's helpful to break down each season, even each change within that season in order to see either the changes that were made to remain successful or the times when the fish fooled you. Be careful to avoid one pitfall that derailed us for a time. By simply plugging each success into each similar situation and avoiding each failed approach we became locked into our own system. That mistake really stalls the learning process. One must continue to experiment and modify the approach to various situations in order to continue improving the results. Most often it's best to use the collected information to duplicate previous successes under the existing conditions but don't neglect thinking outside the box.

## Spring Solutions

First, let's examine the early spring when water temperatures are still pretty cold. After launching a car-top boat on a pretty afternoon at a 30-acre watershed pond the water temperature was checked. It was 52 degrees in three feet of water. A small silt-bottomed cove was lined with willows on one bank and pasture grasses on the other. A point with a decayed weedline guarded the cove's entrance and the main pond's basin that lay beyond it. There was a deadfall extending into eight feet of water on the treed side and a progressively shallow flat with scattered dead weeds on the other. We suspected that crappies were located either just outside this spawning cove or somewhere within it and immediately turned on our flasher unit locator to confirm the suspicion. Using an electric trolling motor we traversed the mouth of the cove twice, noting several isolated fish near the 18-foot bottom. Convinced they weren't crappies we scoped out the little point but found nothing. Next, we ran our locator near and over the deep edge of the deadfall. Again widely scattered "blips" on the unit indicated either widely scattered crappies or possibly other species. We decided against running up on the flat but suspected at least a few crappies were using some portion of it. The flat extended gradually to a depth of about 10 feet. The length of the flat was 40 yards more or less until it reached the back of the cove, which was uniformly shallow and brushy where a tiny intermittent creek entered. Keeping the boat over deep water we pitched small streamers into 4 feet of water, counted them down to near bottom and slowly stripped them back without a hit. Finally, nearly halfway into the cove, a lusty 9-incher was lifted aboard. Dropping anchor, we continued to fan-cast that area and found crappies scattered along the deep edge of the flat willing to bite. We lifted and reset the anchor several times over the next couple of hours, eventually boating and releasing 17 crappies between the two of us. As the sun ducked behind a building bank of clouds the breeze seemed suddenly harsh and we moved out of the cove where we decided to search for the deep fish we had encountered on the locator at the beginning of the day. We found several scattered fish suspended and extended our leaders so we could drift the area at that depth. It took 15 to 20 minutes but finally one small crappie was caught from that area. Another 20 minutes of probing proved fruitless so we returned to our launch site.

Before abandoning the early spring let's visit a sprawling 25,000-acre reservoir in the lower Midwest. After launching on a brisk, breezy afternoon the water temperature was discovered to be 49 degrees. The search began off main lake points and proceeded through areas of confined open water without so much as a single blip on the locator screen. Finally on the inside bend of a brush-covered point the locator came to life. Crappies were suspended horizontally to the brush pile between 12 and 16 feet deep over a 27-foot bottom. Using the electric motor we employed the controlled drift and counted a full-sink line, short 4-foot leaders, and Squirrel Spins to a depth of 10 feet. A double hookup on the first pass made success seem easy but a dozen more methodical drifts later produced only three more fish. Furthermore, the locator was showing fewer fish with each pass. Expanding the search in ever-widening circles finally located fish hovering above the brush pile and still others on the deep edge of the flat that extended far into the cove. With most of the crappies between six and nine feet we made a switch to floating line, long leaders, and size-10 Mini Minnies. In our excitement we fished too fast at first before realizing that the fish were still overpowered by upper-40-degree water. When we slowed our approach and employed a gentle lift, drop, strip retrieve the action picked up. Another 23 fish ,including several of 11 to 12 inches, were caught and released before the late-afternoon chill sent us to the landing.

## Pre-Spawn

One evening we met a friend at a 180-acre lake owned by a small city. It drew lots of picnickers, hikers, and bank-bound catfish tight-liners but few who actively pursued the prolific crappie population. We launched our boat at 4 p.m. and hurried to a favorite spawning cove. The water temperature was 58 degrees and we began casting small streamers toward the brush-covered flat as the electric motor eased us along. The action was nearly constant, but frequent hang-ups forced the use of weed guards. Deep into the cove was a small brush-lined cut that was full of crappies. We anchored on the outside and fan-cast the area where we caught several. Our guest picked up a 14-inch fish on the deep edge of the flat. Near dark we landed at the boat ramp and concluded that the three of us had caught and released 90 crappies.

Some years ago we drove along a large river and stopped at a small pumping station which drained hundreds of acres of crop land. The drainage ditches converged at the pump house where the excess water emptied into the river. Years of the process had created a 40-yard-wide cove of still water which opened into the river's current. A beaver-toppled sycamore extended into the water and a pile of washed-in brush guarded the mouth of the cove. In the dark, stained waters movements could be detected against a shoreline protected by a pile of logs. Perched precariously on the log jam we cast and retrieved Sponge Spiders to within inches of shore and caught three dozen crappies before the action slowed. Moving to the shallow branches of the deadfall and brush we proceeded to catch another dozen on bead-head Woolly Buggers before darkness sent us home.

## Post-Spawn

Let's visit a borrow pit that extends 300 yards along the base of a levy. The maximum depth is eight feet with deadfalls and submerged stumps in one end, a cluster of stumps near the center, and a large deadfall on either side of the 40-yard-wide pit near the far end. On a beautiful mid-70-degree evening we launched two belly boats and paddled to a shallow, sand-bottomed corner to cast small streamers. After catching and quickly releasing 4 nest-guarding males we abandoned the shallows and paddled to within a short cast of the nearby deadfalls and stumps. We each tied on Crappie Bullys. Slowly lifting our flies through the wood pile produced slow but steady fishing for scattered females and one short nose gar that challenged our catch-and-release tactics. We eased ashore and tossed the float tubes in the back of our pickup after releasing a total of 24 fish.

As the spawning season grinds to a halt let's take a look at an 1,800-acre natural lake. It's ringed with bulrushes and a bay that extends away from the sandy beach and a line of boat docks belonging to a fishing resort with several cabins. A quick reconnaissance of the first drop-off outside the weeds showed scattered clusters of fish suspended from six to 12 feet over an irregular bottom of 15 to 20 feet. We decided that since the crappies were scattered, trolling might be the best approach. We used Clouser Deep Minnows and Squirrel Spin but the fish seemed to be disinterested and we had but three in the boat after nearly an hour. As the breeze drifted us away from the bay and along the row of docks in front of the cabins we switched to Woolly Buggers and Crappie Bullys, which immediately produced a double hookup. A couple hours of methodically casting to each dock put another 27 crappies in the boat, including seven that exceeded 12 inches.

# Fooled

All fishermen have days when they are forced to wonder about the sudden disappearance of the fish or why they've acquired lockjaw. After all, we can only make educated guesses as to their location and what might entice them to strike. Our diary reveals our fair share of disappointing results. Here's a sample: One early June afternoon we were camped in a beautiful east Texas State Park. The little lake was well known as a crappie factory so we launched our canoe rigged with a small electric motor and trolled the edge of a deep weedline. Almost immediately a Clouser was slammed by a strong fish that we assumed was a bass. After what seemed a long struggle we lifted a 15-inch crappie aboard. Clearly we had arrived at the right time and the expectation was for big numbers of these strong crappies. It didn't happen. We trolled the weedline relentlessly, cast to a couple of deadfalls, and the long fishing pier that jutted into the lake's deep water. But as darkness approached we hadn't caught another fish. At our campfire that evening we wondered if the big crappie caught and released minutes after starting had been a figment of our imaginations.

On another occasion we invited a friend to join us at a reservoir where just the evening before we had boated 46 from a line of standing timber that hugged the submerged river channel. Using the same flies and tactics that had produced such great fishing less than 24 hours before proved absolutely fruitless. We changed flies and presentations without a fish. Eventually two rather small bluegills were boated on nymphs drifted over the area below a strike indicator, but not one single crappie. Back at the boat ramp we encountered a pair of fishermen that lifted up a stringer of 15 crappies. They had been using spinning gear and live minnows but we hadn't found the crappies despite our ever-widening search with the locator. The two anglers said they had caught the fish between noon and 4 o'clock that the crappies had "just quit biting," and they hadn't landed any since. What had happened? They, and we, had no idea. Sometimes you just have to chalk up the experience as paying your dues.

## Summertime Problem-Solving

Next, let's fish a mid-South reservoir with a strong reputation for producing hefty stringers of crappies. The water temperature is in the mid-80's and the sun is still above the tree line in the late afternoon. We launched our float tubes wearing shorts, wading boots, and fins in a cove where the conservation department has set several large brush piles along the shoreline in 12 to 18 feet of water with their tops rising to within six feet of the surface. Crappie bites were few until the sun dipped beneath the towering trees on the hillside above us. Finally, with the brush pile bathed in shade, our casts to the sides of the brush piles began to connect. We alternated between Crappie Bullys, marabou jigs, and bead-head Woolly Buggers. As sunset approached we cast over the tops of the brush and counted our offerings toward the brush. Most bites came as the flies sank. A yellow/olive tailed Woolly Bugger accounted for the most fish, but the two hefty 12-inchers that won big-fish honors smacked a Crappie Bully on the deep side of the submerged brush. Together we accounted for 27 crappies and several bluegills from the two brush piles in about three hours.

We visited a large oxbow on a muggy early morning. The water was very warm and still, and we chose to wet-wade a sand-bottomed location where a nearby borrow pit drained into a culvert and under the roadway into the oxbow. The gentle flow figured to oxygenate the stained and shallow backwater and in the process attract minnows and game fish. We cast Brim Reapers and small steamers to the slow eddy created by the flow and caught fish immediately. It proved to be a mixed bag with largemouth bass and bluegills sharing the area with the crappies. Wading a bit deeper we soon discovered that the bigger fish tended to flank the small current seam line created by the water's flow. By casting into the seam and allowing our flies to dead-drift into the edge of still water we caught and released several 10-inch crappies and a 15-inch bass. The bonanza was short-lived as the blazing sun intensified and the feeding fish disappeared. Often in the heat of mid-summer the early morning hours provide the best action because the overnight hours enable the water to cool to its lowest temperature of the day and the low light encourages fish to feed.

Switching back to a popular reservoir we used the locator to find crappies suspended in confined open water. With bright sun glaring off the water's surface the crappies were located in a narrow band of depths between 16 and 18 feet. The crappies ignored our offerings on several deep trolling passes so we changed reel spools and rigged for slip-bobber fishing. Setting the depth at 15 feet we lowered our Bass Bullys and Crappie Bullys into the depths and controlled our breeze-blown drifts with the electric motor. These fish apparently had to be bumped on the nose to induce a strike. Fishing was slow at first. We had boated only three in the first hour but when the sun finally began to sink toward the western horizon the crappies moved shallower and became more aggressive. Some of the crappies moved to within eight feet of the surface. We switched to trolling with small Clousers and in the last 30 minutes before nightfall we boated 14 to raise our total to 31. Had we chosen to stay and fish into the night the action would likely have accelerated even further.

Before abandoning summer let's visit a northern natural lake. The week before we had found crappies suspended near bottom at 14 feet off the first breakline. It was the day after a thunderstorm and the fish were very tight-lipped. The past week, however, was warm and sunny. We hoped the crappies would be in a more positive frame of mind. We checked the deep side of the weedline but a few scattered fish indicated a strong possibility of another species. Suspecting that the crappies were inside the weedline we began casting Woolly Buggers, jig flies, and Brim Reapers into pockets in the weeds and allowing them to fall five to six feet. We started catching fish right away and continued to move from the shorebound weedline to submerged mid-lake humps with scattered weeds with great success. At dark we tethered the boat to our host's dock after catching 75 fish.

## Autumn Puzzles

Just as overnight temperatures began to dip we noticed hatches of mayflies emerging from shallow gravel bars that protruded into the lake. There were no surface feeders so we attached our North Fork Nymph in size 12 and allowed it to sink to bottom in two to three feet of water. Our expectation was that bluegills would be feeding there as we had encountered them in similar situations in the past. The bluegills, however, sometimes fed on the adult mayflies perched on the surface. To our surprise it was a school of crappies that were feasting on the nymphs.

Each time our nymph reached bottom we lifted our rod tips to simulate the nymphs' rise to the surface (a modified version of the Leisenring lift). For over an hour the nonstop action continued. As the competitive urges of the crappie school began to wane, we abandoned the location and cruised similar gravel-bar situations. Some apparently had too much wave action to enable the hatch or may just have prevented our being able to see it but gravel-bar areas that were protected from the wind hosted emerging mayflies.

The next area we located was being used by mostly bluegills and we tried to analyze the difference between the two areas but so far are left to wonder. Sometimes it's bluegills, sometimes it's crappies, but rarely are they mixed in this situation.

A resort owner reported that the reservoir was turning over so we loaded float tubes in the truck bed and headed for a 24-acre pond with a maximum depth of 20 feet. The pond is surrounded by thick growths of coontail that extend to a depth of about six feet. We slipped into our waders, climbed into float tubes and paddled along the outside edge of the healthy weeds. Casting small jig flies and streamers to the edges and into the outside pockets in the weeds we found suspended crappies from two to five feet. An irregularly imparted lift, drop, strip retrieve proved lethal on smaller crappies in the six- to eight-inch range until we drifted into a line of stumps near a drop-off. The area between the stumps and the shoreline weeds produced several larger specimens including one that measured 14 inches. By the time we waded ashore we had caught 48 crappies.

A heavy frost blanketed the lawn one early morning so we poured a second cup of coffee and headed to the tying bench, postponing our intended river trip until late afternoon. It was chilly and a high wind whistled through the tree tops as we entered the river in waders. The water was low and the current had slowed. Dead tree branches that lined the bank were now exposed above the water line and a bright sun assaulted the shallow structure. A gravel-bar deadfall furnished a comfortable respite while we waited for the shadows that would soon spread across the river.

The slow current invited North Fork Nymphs and Soft Hackles to be dead-drifted near the submerged branches. Three bluegills and one small crappie later we knotted Brim Reapers and Crappie Bullys to 4X tippets. Immediately the action picked up and 10 to 13-inch crappies were regularly plucked from the wooded maze. Finally, encased in darkness we crossed the river to a gravel bar and hiked back to the bridge where we'd parked, leaving behind 38 crappies with tiny holes in their lips.

An icy wind gust caused us to shiver as we emerged from a cove on famed Kentucky Lake for a late-season crappie trip. Long hailed as one of the nation's best crappie hotspots we hooked up with an old friend that knew the lake well. His big bass boat roared across the lake to a long point covered with dead milfoil. At the end of the point was a drop off into 35 feet of water which extended for an additional 30 yards before a rock pile rose from the depths to within eight feet of the surface. Inactive crappies were suspended off the sides of the rock pile but several trolling passes failed to interest any of them. We moved to another main lake point with a submerged creek brushing against one side. Several slowly trolled, deep

Clousers and Squirrel Spins brought two jumbo crappies to hand, but other bites weren't forthcoming. Huddling deep in our down vests we returned to the original rock pile and began casting over its top and dropping our flies down the sides. We pulled 7-weights out of the boat's hold and started lobbing Squirrel Spins. Almost every hit came as the fly fluttered off the rocks. Seventeen crappies were finally stringered and later cleaned for our friend's elderly neighbor.

While we could continue reciting past trips, both those that were successful and those we'd prefer not to revisit, we hope these selections from our fishing diary will serve as examples of how we put the pieces of the crappie puzzle together. We believe that any crappie that is catchable on conventional tackle is catchable on a fly rod. Further, we know that if the angler understands the needs of the species, the confined environment the fish live in, and the practical use of their situational flies they will catch crappies most of the time. Certainly we've proven that to our own satisfaction and we hope it's proven to you as well. If so, we urge you not to abandon this marvelous species after the spawn but to continue to pursue them in each season. The pursuit is almost certain to capture your heart and may become a delicious obsession.

*Herons can signal minnows feeding near the water's surface.*
*Crappies might be attracted to the easy banquet.*

# Bibliography

Bates, Joseph D. Jr. *Streamer Fly Tying and Fishing*. Harrisburg, Pennsylvania: The Stackpole Company. First Edition 1950 and 1966.

Brooks, Joe. *The Complete Book of Fly Fishing*. U.S.A., 1968

Cutter, Ralph. *Fish Food: A Fly Fisher's Guide to Bugs and Bait*. Mechanicsburg, Pennsylvania: Stackpole Books, 2005.

Ellis, Jack. *The Sunfishes: A Fly Fishing Journey of Discovery*. Bennington, Vermont: Abenaki Publishers, Inc., 1993.

Gapen, Dan D. *Crappie: A Fish for All Seasons*. Big Lake, Minnesota, 1974.

Hauptman, Cliff. *The Fly Fisher's Guide to Warmwater Lakes*. New York: Lyons and Burford, 1995.

Kreiger, Mel. *The Essence of Fly-casting*. San Francisco, California: Club Pacific, 1987.

Leonard, J. Edson. *Flies*. Cranbury, New Jersey: A. S. Barnes and Company, Inc., 1950.

McClane, A. J., ed. *McClane's Standard Fishing Encyclopedia*. New York: Holt, Rinehart, and Winston, 1965.

Meyer, Deke. *Float Tube Fly Fishing*. Portland, Oregon: Frank Amato Publications, Inc., 1989.

Meyer, Deke. *Flyfishing Inflatables*. Portland, Oregon: River Graphics, 1999.

Nemes, Sylvester. *The Soft-Hackled Fly*. Old Greenwich, Connecticut: The Chatham Press, 1975.

Nemes, Sylvester. *Two Centuries of Soft-Hackled Flies*. Mechanicsburg, Pennsylvania: Stackpole Books, 2004.

Nixon, Tom. *Fly Tying and Fly Fishing for Bass and Panfish*. Cranbury, New Jersey: A. S. Barnes and Co., Inc, 1968.

Reynolds, Barry and John Berryman. *Beyond Trout: A Flyfishing Guide*. Boulder, Colorado: Johnson Publishing Company, 1995.

Schwiebert, Ernest. *Nymphs*. Tulsa, Oklahoma: Winchester Press, 1973.

Sosin, Mark and Lefty Kreh. *Practical Fishing Knots*. New York: Lyons and Burford, Publishers, 1991.

Stewart, Dick and Farrow Allen. *Flies for Bass and Panfish*. Intervale, New Hampshire: Northland Press, 1992.

Schollmeyer, Jim. *Patent Patterns*. Portland, Oregon: Frank Amato Publications, Inc., 2003.

# Index

# Index

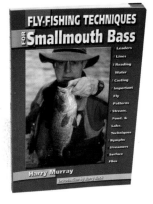